Teach Yourself VISUALLY™

Windows® 8 Tablets

Visual™

by Paul McFedries

WILEY

John Wiley & Sons, Inc.

Teach Yourself VISUALLY™ Windows® 8 Tablets

Published by
John Wiley & Sons, Inc.
10475 Crosspoint Boulevard
Indianapolis, IN 46256

www.wiley.com

Published simultaneously in Canada

Wiley publishes in a variety of print and electronic formats and by print-on-demand. Some material included with standard print versions of this book may not be included in e-books or in print-on-demand. If this book refers to media such as a CD or DVD that is not included in the version you purchased, you may download this material at http://booksupport.wiley.com. For more information about Wiley products, visit www.wiley.com.

Library of Congress Control Number: 2012947688

ISBN: 978-1-118-37485-6 (paperback); 978-1-118-49129-4 (epdf); 978-1-118-46395-6 (emobi); 978-1-118-46394-9 (epub)

Manufactured in the United States of America

10 9 8 7 6 5 4 3 2 1

Trademark Acknowledgments

Contact Us

For general information on our other products and services, please contact our Customer Care Department within the U.S. at (877)762-2974, outside the United States at (317)572-3993, or fax (317)572-4002.

For technical support, please visit www.wiley.com/techsupport.

WILEY   Sales | Contact Wiley at (877) 762-2974 or fax (317) 572-4002.

Credits

Acquisitions Editor
Aaron Black

Project Editor
Dana Rhodes Lesh

Technical Editor
Vince Averello

Copy Editor
Dana Rhodes Lesh

Editorial Director
Robyn Siesky

Business Manager
Amy Knies

Senior Marketing Manager
Sandy Smith

Vice President and Executive Group Publisher
Richard Swadley

Vice President and Executive Publisher
Barry Pruett

Project Coordinator
Sheree Montgomery

Graphics and Production Specialists
Carrie A. Cesavice
Jennifer Henry
Andrea Hornberger
Sennett Johnson
Jill A. Proll

Quality Control Technicians
John Greenough
Susan Moritz

Proofreading and Indexing
BIM Indexing & Proofreading Services

About the Author

Paul McFedries is a full-time technical writer. Paul has been authoring computer books since 1991 and has more than 75 books to his credit. His books have sold more than four million copies worldwide. These books include the Wiley titles *Windows 8 Visual Quick Tips*, *The Facebook Guide for People Over 50*, *iPhone 4S Portable Genius*, and *The New iPad Portable Genius*. Paul is also the proprietor of Word Spy (www.wordspy.com), a website that tracks new words and phrases as they enter the language. Paul invites you to drop by his personal website at www.mcfedries.com or follow him on Twitter at @paulmcf and @wordspy.

Author's Acknowledgments

It goes without saying that writers focus on text, and I certainly enjoyed focusing on the text that you will read in this book. However, this book is more than just the usual collection of words and phrases. A quick thumbthrough the pages will show you that this book is also chock-full of images, from sharp screenshots to fun and informative illustrations. Those colorful images make for a beautiful book, and that beauty comes from a lot of hard work by Wiley's immensely talented group of designers and layout artists. They are all listed in the Credits section on the previous page, and I thank them for creating another gem. Of course, what you read in this book must also be accurate, logically presented, and free of errors. Ensuring all of this was an excellent group of editors that included project editor and copy editor Dana Lesh and technical editor Vince Averello. Thanks for your exceptional competence and hard work. Thanks, as well, to Wiley acquisitions editor Aaron Black for asking me to write this book.

How to Use This Book

Whom This Book Is For

This book is for the reader who has never used a Windows 8 tablet. It is also for readers who want to expand their knowledge of Windows.

The Conventions in This Book

❶ Steps

This book uses a step-by-step format to guide you easily through each task. Numbered steps are actions you must perform; bulleted steps clarify a point, step, or optional feature; and indented steps give you the result.

❷ Notes

Notes give additional information — special conditions that may occur during an operation, a situation that you want to avoid, or a cross-reference to a related area of the book.

❸ Icons and Buttons

Icons and buttons show you exactly what you need to tap to perform a step.

❹ Tips

Tips offer additional information, including warnings and shortcuts.

❺ Bold

Bold type shows command names or options that you must tap or text or numbers you must type.

❻ Italics

Italic type introduces and defines a new term.

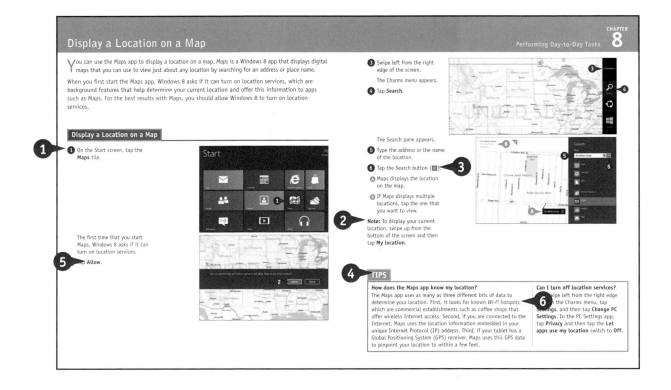

Table of Contents

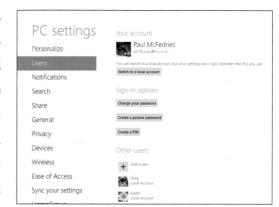

Table of Contents

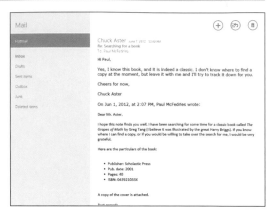

Chapter 6   Getting Social with Your Tablet

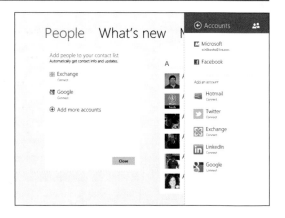

Chapter 7	Working with Multimedia

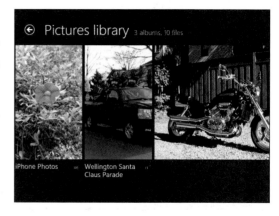

Table of Contents

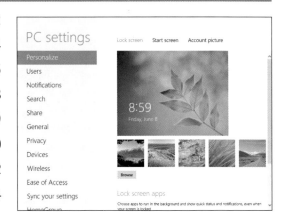

Chapter 10 | Creating and Editing Documents

Chapter 11 | Working with Files

Table of Contents

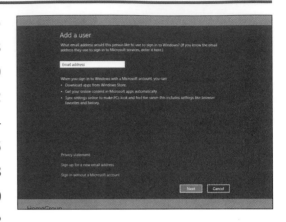

Chapter 14 Maintaining Windows 8

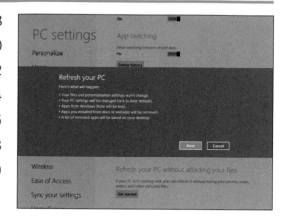

CHAPTER 1

Getting Started with Windows 8

Are you ready to discover the Windows 8 tablet? In this chapter, you take a tour of Windows 8, learn about gestures, and learn how to start and shut down Windows 8.

Start Windows 8

When you turn on your tablet, Windows 8 starts automatically, but you may have to navigate the sign-on screen along the way.

To prevent other people from using your tablet without your authorization, Windows 8 requires you to set up a username and password. You supply this information the very first time you start your tablet, when Windows 8 takes you through a series of configuration steps. Each time you start your tablet, Windows 8 presents the sign-on screen, and you must enter your username and password to continue.

Start Windows 8

1 Turn on your tablet.

After a few seconds, the Windows 8 lock screen appears.

2 Place a finger or a stylus on the screen, slide up an inch or two, and then release the screen.

Note: See "Understanding Gestures," later in this chapter, to learn more about using touch input with your Windows 8 tablet.

The Windows 8 sign-on screen appears.

3 Tap inside the **Password** box.

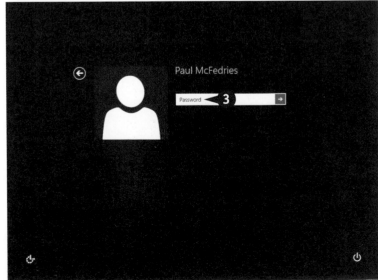

Ⓐ Windows 8 displays the touch keyboard.

④ Type your password.

Note: See "Input Text with the Touch Keyboard" for more information on the touch keyboard.

⑤ Tap the Submit arrow (→).

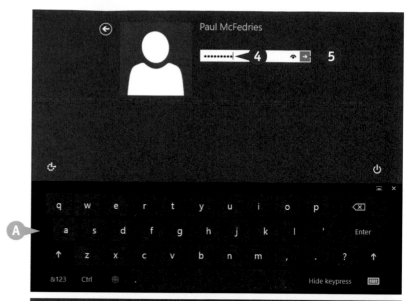

The Windows 8 Start screen appears.

TIPS

When I type my password in the sign-on screen, how can I be sure that I am typing the correct characters?

For added security, when you type your password, the characters appear as dots so that someone who is nearby cannot read your password. If you know that there is no danger of someone reading your password, tap and hold the Display Password Characters icon (👁). This changes the dots to the actual characters. When you release the screen, the characters return to dots.

Windows 8 "lights up" each key as I tap it. Would it not be possible for someone to determine my password by following these taps?

In theory, yes, this is possible. If you are using your Windows 8 tablet in a public location or if you think that there is a possibility that someone might see your password taps, tap the **Hide keypress** key on the keyboard. This prevents Windows 8 from lighting up each key as you tap it.

Explore the Windows 8 Start Screen

Before getting to the specifics of working with Windows 8, take a few seconds to familiarize yourself with the basic elements of the Start screen. These elements include the Start screen's app tiles, live tiles, your user tile, and the Desktop tile.

Understanding where these elements appear on the Start screen and what they are used for will help you work through the rest of this book and will help you navigate Windows 8 and its applications on your own.

Ⓐ Tile

Each of these rectangles represents an app or a Windows 8 feature. Most of the programs that you install will add their own tiles to the Start screen.

Ⓑ User Tile

You use this tile to access features related to your Windows 8 user account.

Ⓒ Live Tile

Some tiles are *live* in the sense that they display frequently updated information, such as the current weather shown by the Weather tile and the stock data shown by the Finance tile.

Display the Charms Menu

You can access many of the Windows 8 options, settings, and features by displaying the Charms menu.

One of the design goals of Windows 8 was to keep the screen simple and uncluttered. Therefore, the Start screen displays no menus, toolbars, or other elements that are normally associated with computer programs. Instead, you access these extra elements using gestures. One of the most useful of these extra elements is the Charms menu.

Display the Charms Menu

1 Place your finger or your tablet stylus on the right edge of the screen.

2 Swipe your finger or the stylus along the screen to the left for an inch or two.

Note: See "Understanding Gestures," later in this chapter, to learn more about using touch input with your Windows 8 tablet.

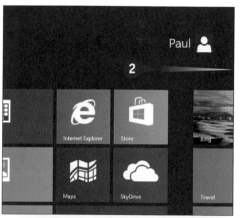

Windows 8 displays the Charms menu.

A You tap **Search** to locate apps, settings, or files on your tablet.

B You tap **Share** to send data from your tablet to other people.

C You tap **Start** to return to the Start screen when you are using an app.

D You tap **Devices** to see a list of devices installed on your tablet.

E You tap **Settings** to adjust the Windows 8 options.

Get to Know the Windows 8 Apps

You can get up to speed quickly with Windows 8 by understanding what each of the default Start screen tiles represents and what you use them for.

Most of the Start screen tiles are *apps* — short for *applications* — which are programs that you use to work, play, and get things done with Windows 8.

A Mail
You use this app to send and receive e-mail messages.

B Calendar
You use this app to schedule appointments, meetings, and other events.

C Photos
You use this app to view the photos and other pictures that you have on your tablet.

D Finance
You can use this app to track stocks, get financial news, and more.

E Weather
You use this app to get the latest weather and forecast for one or more cities.

F Desktop
This app represents the Windows 8 desktop.

G Messaging
This app enables you to send text messages.

H People
This app connects you with the people in your life by enabling you to store contact data, connect with your Facebook and Twitter accounts, and more.

A Internet Explorer

You use this app to navigate sites on the World Wide Web (WWW).

B Store

This tile represents the Windows Store, which you can use to install more apps.

C Bing

This tile opens the Bing search engine, which you can use to search for information on the World Wide Web.

D Travel

This app enables you to research destinations, plan a trip, and book flights and hotel rooms.

E Camera

This app connects with your tablet's camera to take a picture or video.

F Video

This app lets you watch the videos and movies stored on your tablet, as well as buy or rent movies and TV shows.

G Music

This app lets you play the music files on your tablet, as well as purchase music.

H News

You can use this app to read the latest news in categories such as politics, technology, and entertainment.

I Games

This app lets you download games that you can play on either your tablet or your Xbox gaming console.

J Sports

You can use this app to get the latest sports schedules and scores, follow your favorite teams, view standings and statistics, and more.

K SkyDrive

You can use this app to send files to your SkyDrive, which is an online storage area associated with your Microsoft account.

L Maps

This app shows you locations on a map and provides directions.

Understanding Gestures

You can get the most out of your Windows 8 tablet by learning the various gestures that you can use to initiate actions, manipulate data, and control the elements on your screen.

Traditional computers use the mouse and keyboard to input data and make things happen. A tablet lacks these input devices; instead you must rely on your fingers because tablets are built to respond to touches on the glass screen surface. Some tablets also come with a small pen-like device called a *stylus,* which you can use instead of your finger for some actions.

Tap

Use your finger to touch the screen and then immediately release it. You use this gesture to initiate an action.

Double-Tap

Tap and release the screen twice, one tap right after the other. You also use this gesture to initiate an action, although mostly with older desktop programs.

Tap and Hold

Press your finger on the screen for a second or two. This gesture usually displays a menu of options related to whatever screen object you are pressing.

Slide

Place your finger on the screen, move your finger, and then release. You use this gesture either to move an object from one place to another or to scroll the screen in the same direction as your finger.

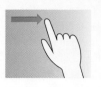

Swipe

Quickly and briefly run your finger along the screen. This gesture is often used to select an object, but there are also specific swipe gestures that display screen elements. See "Display the Charms Menu" for an example.

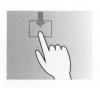

Pinch

Place two fingers apart on the screen and bring them closer together. This gesture zooms out on whatever is displayed on the screen, such as a photo.

Spread

Place two fingers close together on the screen and move them farther apart. This gesture zooms in on whatever is displayed on the screen, such as a photo.

Turn

Place two fingers on the screen and turn them clockwise or counterclockwise. This gesture rotates whatever is displayed on the screen, such as a photo.

Using Gestures to Control Windows 8

To use your tablet efficiently and accurately, you need to know how to use gestures to control Windows 8. Using a tablet is a different experience than using a regular computer, but Windows 8 was built with the tablet in mind, so it is intuitive and easy to learn.

If you have never used a tablet PC before, the main difference is that you use your fingers (or stylus) to run applications, select items, and manipulate screen objects. This might seem awkward at first, but it will come to seem quite natural if you practice the techniques shown here as much as you can.

Using Gestures to Control Windows 8

Initiate an Action

1 Position your finger or the stylus over the object that you want to work with.

2 Tap the screen.

Depending on the object, Windows 8 either selects the object or performs some operation in response to the tap, such as displaying the Desktop.

Swipe the Screen

1 Quickly move your finger or the stylus across the screen, as follows:

• Swipe left from the right edge of the tablet to display the Charms menu.

• Swipe right from the left edge of the tablet to switch between running applications.

• If an application takes up multiple screens, swipe right or left to navigate the screens.

• Swipe down on a tile to select it.

A When you select a tile, Windows 8 displays its related commands.

Display the Application Bar

1 Place your finger or stylus at the bottom edge of the screen.

2 Swipe up.

B Windows 8 displays the application bar.

Note: The application bar's contents vary depending on the app you are using.

Move an Item

1 Position your finger or the stylus over the item that you want to move.

2 Tap and hold the item and immediately begin moving your finger or the stylus.

The object moves along with your finger or the stylus.

3 When the object is repositioned where you want it, lift your finger or the stylus off the screen to complete the move.

TIP

After I tap an app tile, how do I return to the Start screen?

There are a couple of ways that you can do this:

- Display the Charms menu and then tap **Start**. For more information, see the section "Display the Charms Menu" earlier in this chapter.
- Display the list of running apps and then tap the Start thumbnail. For more information, see the section "Switch between Apps" in Chapter 2.
- Close the app. For more details, see the section "Close an App" in Chapter 2.

Input Text with the Touch Keyboard

If you are using a Windows 8 tablet, or a Windows 8 tablet PC in tablet mode, you do not have a physical keyboard available. To input text, Windows 8 offers the touch keyboard, which is a virtual keyboard that appears on the screen. You input text using this keyboard by tapping the keys. Windows 8 offers several touch keyboard types, and some characters are difficult to find, so you need to know how to use the touch keyboard to get the most out of Windows 8.

Input Text with the Touch Keyboard

Select a Keyboard

1 In an app, tap the text box area in which you want text to be inserted.

A Windows 8 displays the touch keyboard.

2 Tap ▦.

Windows 8 displays the keyboard options.

B Tap ▦ for the regular keyboard.

C Tap ▦ for the split keyboard.

D Tap ☑ for the writing pad.

Note: See the Tip for more information.

E Tap ⬛ to hide the keyboard.

Input Text

1 Use the keys to tap the characters that you want to input.

Windows 8 inserts the text.

F To enter an uppercase letter, tap Shift (⬛) and then tap the letter.

G To delete the previous character, tap Backspace (⬛).

2 To enter numbers and other symbols, tap ⬛.

Windows 8 displays the numbers and symbols.

3 Tap ⊙ to see more symbols.

4 To see more symbols, tap and hold a key.

H Windows 8 displays the extra symbols.

5 Slide your finger to the symbol that you want and then release.

I Tap ⊖ to return to the previous symbols.

J Tap ▦ to return to the letters.

6 When you are done, tap ▦ and then tap 🖵 to hide the keyboard.

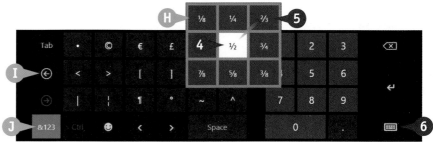

TIP

How do I write text with the stylus?

If your tablet comes with a stylus, you can use it to write text directly on the screen instead of tapping the touch keyboard. Follow these steps:

1 Follow steps **1** and **2** in the "Select a Keyboard" subsection and then tap ▱.

Windows 8 displays the writing pad.

2 Use the stylus to handwrite the text in the writing pad.

A After a few seconds, Windows 8 converts your writing to text.

3 Repeat step **2** until you are ready to insert the text.

4 Tap **Insert**.

Windows 8 inserts the text.

5 Repeat steps **2** to **4** to add the rest of your text.

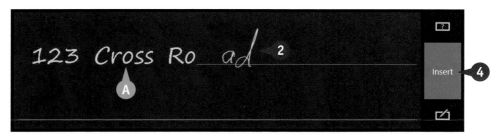

Connect to a Wireless Network

If you have a wireless access point and your tablet has built-in wireless networking capabilities, you can connect to the wireless access point to access your network. If your wireless access point is connected to the Internet, then connecting to the wireless network gives your tablet Internet access, as well.

Most wireless networks are protected with a security key, which is a kind of password. Make sure that you know the key before attempting to connect. However, after you have connected to the network once, Windows 8 remembers the password and connects again automatically whenever the network comes within range.

Connect to a Wireless Network

1 Display the Charms menu and then tap **Settings**.

Note: See the section "Display the Charms Menu" earlier in this chapter.

The Settings pane appears.

2 Tap the Network icon (📶).

A Windows 8 displays a list of wireless networks in your area.

3 Tap your network.

4 To have Windows 8 connect to your network automatically in the future, tap to activate the **Connect automatically** check box (☐ changes to ☑).

5 Tap **Connect**.

If the network is protected by a security key, Windows 8 prompts you to enter it.

6 Type the security key.

B If you want to be certain that you typed the security key correctly, temporarily tap and hold ⟨⟩.

7 Tap **Next**.

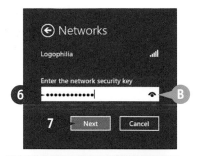

Windows 8 connects to the network.

8 Display the Charms menu and then tap **Settings**.

C The network icon changes from ⚹⃒ to ⚹⃒ to indicate that you now have a wireless network connection.

TIP

How do I disconnect from my wireless network?
To disconnect from the network, follow these steps:

1 Display the Charms menu and then tap **Settings**.

2 Tap ⚹⃒.

3 Tap your network.

4 Tap **Disconnect**.

Windows 8 disconnects from the wireless network.

Create a Microsoft Account

You can get much more out of Windows 8 by using a Microsoft account. When you connect a Microsoft account to your Windows 8 user account, many previously inaccessible Windows 8 features become immediately available. For example, you can use the Mail app to access your e-mail and the Messages app to exchange text messages with other Microsoft account users.

You can also download apps from the Windows Store, access your photos and documents anywhere online, and even sync your settings with other PCs or tablets for which you use the same account.

Create a Microsoft Account

Start the Creation of a Microsoft Account

1 Display the Charms menu, tap **Search**, and then tap **Settings**.

Note: See the section "Display the Charms Menu" earlier in this chapter.

The Settings search pane appears.

2 Type **microsoft**.

Windows 8 displays the "microsoft" search results.

3 Tap **Connect to a Microsoft account**.

Windows 8 displays the PC Settings window with the Users tab selected.

4 Tap **Switch to a Microsoft account**.

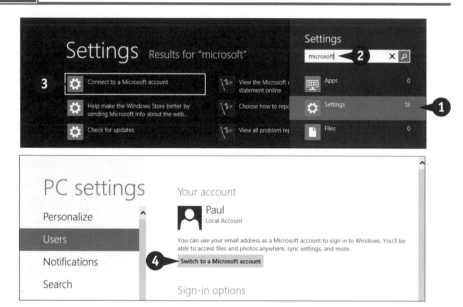

Windows 8 asks you to verify your current account password.

5 Type your password.

6 Tap **Next**.

Windows 8 asks you to enter your e-mail address.

7 Type your e-mail address.

8 Tap **Next**.

TIPS

How do I create a new account using either Windows Live or Hotmail?

When you type the e-mail address, type the username that you prefer to use, followed by either **live.com** or **hotmail. com**. If the username has not been taken, Windows 8 will recognize that this is a new address, and it will create the new account automatically.

Can I use a non-Microsoft e-mail address?

Yes, you can. Windows 8 does not require that you use a Windows Live or Hotmail e-mail address from Microsoft. If you have an e-mail address that you use regularly, you are free to use that with your Windows 8 account.

continued ▶

How you proceed after you type your e-mail address depends on whether you are creating a new Microsoft account or using an existing account. Using a Microsoft account with Windows 8 can help if you forget your account password and cannot log in.

You can provide Microsoft with your mobile phone number, so if you ever forget your password, Microsoft will send you a text message to help you reset your password. You can also give Microsoft an alternative e-mail address, or you can provide the answer to a secret question.

Create a Microsoft Account (continued)

Configure a New Microsoft Account

The account information page appears.

Note: If you are configuring an existing Microsoft account, skip to the next subsection.

1 Type your password in both text boxes.

2 Type your first name.

3 Type your last name.

4 Choose your country.

5 Type your zip code.

6 Tap **Next**.

Note: From here, continue with the "Complete the Account" subsection.

Configure an Existing Microsoft Account

1 Type your Microsoft account password.

2 Tap **Next**.

Complete the Account

The Add Security Verification Info page appears.

1 Type your mobile phone number.

2 Type an alternate e-mail address.

3 Choose a secret question.

4 Type the answer to the question.

5 Tap **Next**.

If you are creating a new account, Windows 8 asks for some extra information.

6 Choose the month, date, and year of your birth.

7 Tap either **Male** or **Female** (○ changes to ◉).

8 Type the characters that you see in the box.

9 Tap the check box (☑ changes to ☐).

10 Tap **Next**.

11 Tap **Finish**.

Windows 8 connects the Microsoft account to your user account.

The next time you start Windows 8, use your Microsoft account e-mail address and password to log in.

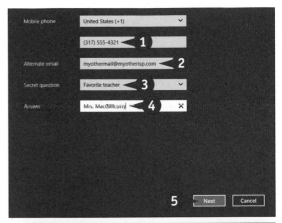

TIP

If I no longer want to use a Microsoft account with Windows 8, can I remove it?

Yes, you can revert to using your original user account at any time. Note, however, that you will no longer see any personal data on the Start screen, you will not be able to access your files online, and your settings will no longer sync between PCs.

To remove the Microsoft account, display the Charms menu, tap **Search**, and then tap **Settings** to open the Settings search pane, type **microsoft**, and then tap **Disconnect a Microsoft account**. In the PC Settings window, tap **Switch to a local account**.

Type your Microsoft account password, tap **Next**, type your local account password (twice) and a password hint, and tap **Next**. Tap **Sign out and finish** to complete the removal.

Work with Notifications

To keep you informed of events and information related to your tablet, Windows 8 displays notifications, so you need to understand what they are and how to handle them.

As you work with your tablet, certain events and conditions will display a notification on the screen. For example, you might add an appointment to the Calendar app and ask the app to remind you about it. Similarly, someone might send you a text message, or you might insert a USB flash drive, and Windows 8 will question what you want to do with its contents.

Work with Notifications

A When an event occurs on your tablet, such as when you insert a USB flash drive, Windows 8 displays a notification.

1 Tap the notification.

B If you do not want to do anything with the notification at this time, tap ×.

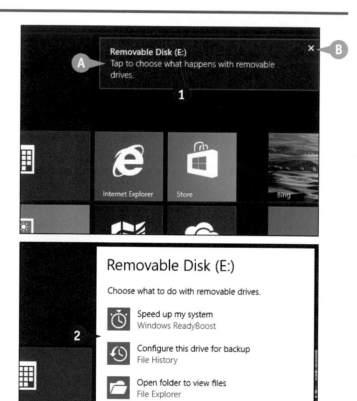

C Windows 8 displays options related to the notification.

2 Tap the option that you want to use.

Windows 8 carries out the task.

Put Windows 8 to Sleep

You can make your tablet more energy efficient by putting Windows 8 into sleep mode when you are not using the tablet. *Sleep mode* means that your tablet is in a temporary low-power mode. This saves electricity when your tablet is plugged in, and it saves battery power when your tablet is unplugged.

In sleep mode, Windows 8 keeps your apps open. This is handy because it means that when you return from sleep mode, after you sign in to Windows 8 again, you can immediately get back to what you were doing.

Put Windows 8 to Sleep

1 Display the Charms menu and then tap **Settings**.

Note: See the section "Display the Charms Menu" earlier in this chapter.

The Settings pane appears.

2 Tap the **Power** button (⏻).

3 Tap **Sleep.**

Windows 8 activates sleep mode.

Note: To return from sleep mode, press your tablet's Power button.

Restart Windows 8

You can restart Windows 8, which means that it shuts down and starts up again immediately. This is useful if your tablet is running slowly or acting funny. Sometimes a restart solves the problem.

Knowing how to restart Windows 8 also comes in handy when you install a program or device that requires a restart to function properly. If you are busy at the time, you can always opt to restart your tablet yourself later, when it is more convenient.

Restart Windows 8

1 Shut down all your running programs.

Note: Be sure to save your work as you close your programs.

2 Display the Charms menu and then tap **Settings**.

Note: See the section "Display the Charms Menu" earlier in this chapter.

The Settings pane appears.

3 Tap 🔌.

4 Tap **Restart**.

Windows 8 shuts down, and your tablet restarts.

Shut Down Windows 8

Whan you complete your work, you should shut down Windows 8. However, you do not want to just shut off your tablet's power. Instead, you should follow the proper steps to avoid damaging files on your system. Shutting off the tablet's power without properly exiting Windows 8 can cause two problems: First, if you have unsaved changes in some open documents, you may lose those changes. Second, you could damage one or more Windows 8 system files, which could make your system unstable.

Shut Down Windows 8

1 Shut down all your running programs.

Note: Be sure to save your work as you close your programs.

2 Display the Charms menu and then tap **Settings**.

Note: See the section "Display the Charms Menu" earlier in this chapter.

The Settings pane appears.

3 Tap 🔵.

4 Tap **Shut down**.

Windows 8 shuts down and turns off your tablet.

CHAPTER 2

Working with Apps

To do something useful with your tablet, you need to work with *apps* — short for *applications* — either ones that come with Windows 8 or ones that you install yourself. In this chapter, you learn how to install, launch, and work with apps.

Store

Games >

Reversi Twist
Free ★★★★☆

Top free

New releases

Get that "Ah-ha!" feeling
Challenging puzzle games

ARMED!
Free ★★★★☆

Paint 4 Kids
Free ★★★★★

Pirates Love Daisies
Free ★★★★☆

Explore the Windows Store

You can use the Windows Store to research and install new apps on your tablet.

The traditional methods for locating and installing new apps are to purchase an app from a retail store or to download an app from the Internet. The retail-store method is inconvenient and time-consuming, and the Internet method is potentially unsafe. A better solution is to use the Windows Store, which is directly accessible from the Windows 8 Start screen. It is fast and efficient, and you always know that you are getting safe apps.

Explore the Windows Store

1 On the Start screen, tap **Store**.

The Windows Store appears.

2 Swipe left and right to navigate the screen.

Ⓐ The category names appear here.

Ⓑ Tap this tile to see a list of the new releases in the category.

Ⓒ Tap this tile to see a list of the most popular free apps in the category.

Ⓓ Tap any other tile to go directly to its app.

3 Tap the category that you want to view.

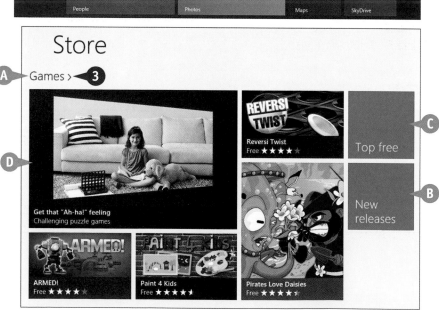

The Windows Store displays the apps in the category that you selected.

E Tap this ⌄ to sort the apps.

F Tap this ⌄ to filter the apps by price.

G If you see the app you want, tap it.

4 Tap this ⌄ and then tap a subcategory.

The Windows Store displays the apps in the subcategory that you selected.

5 Tap an app.

Note: See the next section to learn how to install an app.

H To retrace your steps in the Windows Store, tap the Back button (⊙).

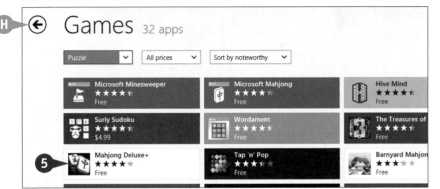

TIP

Is there a way to see just the most recent apps added to the Windows Store?
Yes. When you open the Windows Store, navigate to the **Spotlight** category on the main screen. From there, tap the **New releases** tile (A). The Windows Store displays a list of the apps that have most recently been added to the store.

Install an App

If Windows 8 does not come with an app that you need, you can obtain the app yourself and then install it on your tablet.

How you start the installation process depends on whether you obtained the app from the new Windows Store that comes with Windows 8 or whether you downloaded the app from the Internet. If you purchased the app from a retail store or if you used the WWW to order a physical copy of the software instead of downloading it, you install the app using the CD or DVD disc that comes in the package.

Install an App

Install from the Windows Store

1 On the Start screen, tap **Store**.

The Windows Store appears.

2 Display the app that you want to install.

Note: See the section "Explore the Window Store" to learn how to navigate the store.

3 Tap **Install**.

Windows 8 installs the app.

Install from a File Downloaded from the Internet

1 Swipe left from the right edge of the screen to display the Charms menu and then tap **Search**.

2 On the Start screen, type **downloads**.

Windows 8 displays the "downloads" search results.

3 Tap **Downloads**.

Note: If you saved the downloaded file in a folder other than Downloads, use File Explorer to find the downloaded file. To view a file with File Explorer, see the section "View Your Files" in Chapter 11.

The Downloads folder appears.

4 Double-tap the file.

The software's installation app begins.

Note: For compressed files, extract the files and then double-tap the setup file. See the section "Zip Up and Extract Compressed Files" in Chapter 11.

5 Follow the installation instructions that the app provides.

TIPS

How do I install software from a CD or DVD?
Connect an optical drive to your tablet, if necessary, and then insert the disc. After a moment or two, the AutoPlay notification appears. Tap the notification and then tap **Run** *file*, where *file* is the name of the installation app, usually SETUP.EXE. Then follow the installation instructions that the app provides. Note that these installation steps vary from app to app.

How do I find my software's product key or serial number?
The product key or serial number is crucial because many apps do not install until you enter the number. Look for a sticker attached to the back or inside of the CD case. Also look on the registration card, the CD itself, or the back of the box. If you downloaded the app, the number should appear on the download screen and on the e-mail receipt that you receive.

Start an App

To perform tasks of any kind in Windows 8, you use one of the apps installed on your tablet. The application you use depends on the task that you want to perform. For example, if you want to surf the World Wide Web, you would use a web browser application, such as the Internet Explorer app that comes with Windows 8.

Before you can use an application, however, you must first tell Windows 8 which application you want to run. In Windows 8, you can run selected apps using the Start screen or the Apps screen.

Start an App

Using the Start Screen

1 Tap the tile for the app that you want to launch.

Note: If you have more apps installed than can fit on the main Start screen, scroll to the right and then tap the app tile.

The app runs.

A Certain Windows 8 apps take over the entire screen.

Using the Apps Screen

1 On the Start screen, swipe up from the bottom edge of the screen.

2 Tap **All apps**.

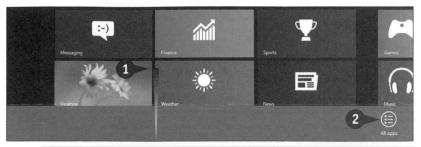

The Apps screen appears.

3 Tap the app that you want to run.

Windows 8 launches the app.

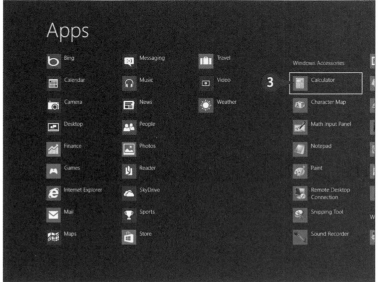

Is there an easier way to locate an app, particularly when the Apps screen has dozens of icons?

Yes, you can perform an Apps search to locate it. Swipe left from the right edge of the screen to display the Charms menu and then tap **Search** to open the Apps search pane. Begin typing the name of the app. As you type, Windows 8 displays a list of apps that match the characters. As soon as you see the app that you want, tap it to run the program.

How can I start an app that does not appear on the Start screen, on the Apps screen, or in the Apps Search results?

Windows 8 comes with some programs that do not appear any of these places. These are mostly Windows 8 tools and utilities, and Windows 8 recognizes these programs based only on their filenames, not their program names. Therefore, use the Apps search pane, as described in the previous Tip, to run a search on the filename, if you know it.

Understanding App Screens

Windows 8 supports two quite different types of apps — the standard Desktop type and a new type of program designed specifically to work with Windows 8 — but on your tablet, you will mostly use the new Windows 8 apps. Windows 8 apps take up the entire screen when they are running, and they hide their program features until you need them.

To get the most out of a Windows 8 app, you need to understand the major features of an app screen.

Ⓐ Application Bar

The application bar contains buttons that give you access to various app features and commands. Note that in some apps, the application bar appears at the top of the screen rather than at the bottom. To display the application bar, either swipe up from the bottom edge of the screen or swipe down from the top edge of the screen.

Ⓑ Toolbar

The toolbar has buttons, lists, and other items that offer easy access to common app commands and features. Some buttons are commands, and some have lists from which you can make a choice. Note that not all Windows 8 apps come with a toolbar. You use the same techniques to display the toolbar as for the application bar.

Ⓒ Settings

The app settings are commands that you can select to configure and customize the app. To display the settings, swipe left from the right edge of the screen to display the Charms menu and then tap **Settings**.

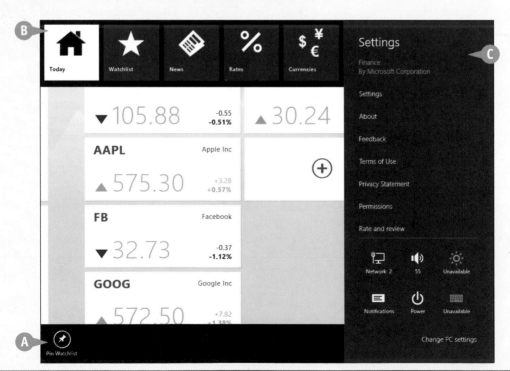

Close an App

In Windows 8, you generally do not need to close an app after you are finished with it. Apps that remain open use very few system resources, so your tablet's performance will not suffer by leaving apps open. However, as you see in the next section, "Switch between Apps," having several apps open can make it more difficult to switch from one to another. When that happens, you should close one or more apps that you are not using, making it easier to switch between others.

Close an App

1 Slide your finger or stylus down from the top edge of the screen to about the middle of the screen.

A Windows 8 reduces the app to this thumbnail version.

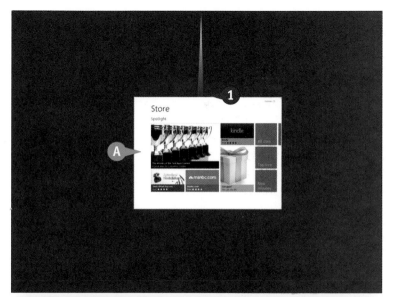

2 Slide your finger or stylus all the way to the bottom edge of the screen.

B Windows 8 displays an even smaller version of the app.

3 Release the screen.

Windows 8 closes the app.

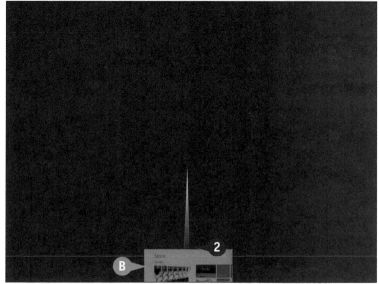

Switch between Apps

In Windows 8, after you start one application, you do not need to close that application before you open another one. Windows 8 supports a feature called *multitasking,* which means running two or more applications at once. If you plan on doing so, you need to know how to easily switch from one application to another. This is handy if you need to use several applications throughout the day. For example, you might keep your word-processing application, your web browser, and your e-mail application open all day.

Switch between Apps

Cycle through the Running Windows 8 Apps

1 Slide a finger or stylus in from the left edge of the screen.

A As you slide, your finger or stylus drags in the next app window.

2 If that is not the app you want, release the screen and repeat step **1**.

3 When you see the app you want, release the screen to switch to that app.

Switch to a Particular Running Windows 8 App

1 Slide a finger or stylus in from the left edge of the screen.

B The next app window appears.

2 Drag the next app window back to the left edge of the screen.

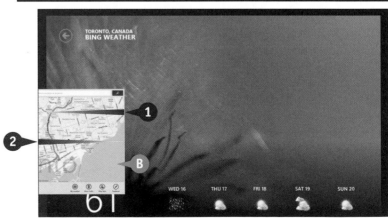

C Windows 8 displays a list of running apps.

3 Tap the app that you want to use.

Switch Desktop Apps Using the Taskbar

1 Tap the taskbar button of the app to which you want to switch.

D You can also switch to another window by tapping the window, even if it is in the background.

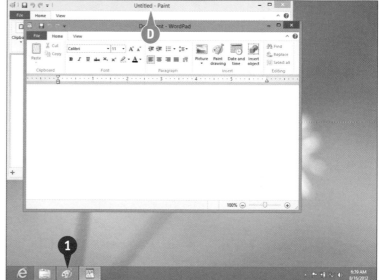

TIP

How do I switch to the Start screen from an app?
Windows 8 gives you two different ways to do this:

• Swipe left from the right edge of the screen to display the Charms menu and then tap **Start**.

• Follow steps **1** and **2** in the "Switch to a Particular Running Windows 8 App" subsection to display the list of running apps and then tap the Start screen thumbnail (A) in the bottom-left corner of the screen.

Update an App

You can ensure that you are using the latest version of an app by using the Windows Store to install an available update.

After a software company releases an app, its programmers continue to work on it. They add new features, improve existing features, fix problems, and close security holes. After fully testing these improvements and fixes, they place the new version of the app in the Windows Store, which alerts you that there is an update. You can then install the new version.

Update an App

1 Switch to the Start screen.

A If you have updated apps available, you see the number of updates here.

2 Tap **Store**.

The Windows Store app appears.

3 Tap **Updates**.

The Windows Store displays a list of the available updates.

Ⓑ If you want to update only some of the apps, tap **Clear**.

Ⓒ If you prefer to update all of the apps at once, tap **Select all** and skip to step **5**.

④ Tap each update that you want to install.

⑤ Tap **Install**.

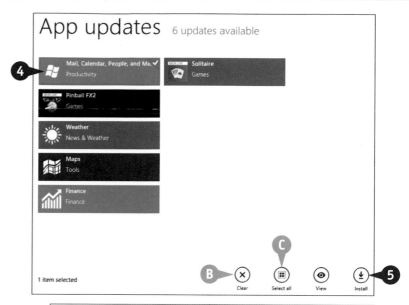

App updates   6 updates available

Windows 8 installs the app updates.

Ⓓ The Windows Store tells you which app is being updated here.

Store

Spotlight

TIP

How do I update Windows 8?

By default, Windows 8 is configured to automatically check for updated system files each day. If any updates are available, Windows 8 downloads and installs them automatically.

If you know of an important update, you can check for it by hand if you would rather not wait for the automatic check. Swipe left from the right edge of the screen to display the Charms menu, tap **Settings**, and then tap **Change PC settings** to open the PC Settings app. At the bottom of the tab list, tap **Windows Update** and then tap **Check for updates now** (A).

Uninstall an App

If you have an app that you no longer use, you can free up some disk space and reduce clutter on the Start screen by uninstalling it.

When you install an app, the program stores its files on your tablet's hard disk, and although most programs are quite small, many require hundreds of megabytes of disk space. Uninstalling an app you do not need frees up the disk space that it uses and removes its tile (or tiles) from the Start screen — if it has any there — and the Apps screen.

Uninstall an App

Uninstall a Windows 8 App

1 Use the Start screen or the Apps screen to locate the Windows 8 app that you want to uninstall.

Note: To display the Apps screen, switch to the Start screen, swipe up from the bottom edge, and then tap **All apps**.

2 Swipe down on the app tile.

Ⓐ Windows 8 displays the application bar.

3 Tap **Uninstall**.

Windows 8 asks you to confirm.

4 Tap **Uninstall**.

Windows 8 removes the app.

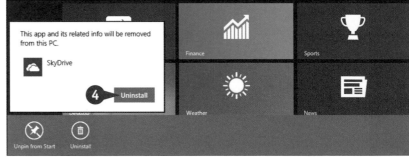

Uninstall a Desktop App

1 Swipe left from the right edge of the screen and then tap **Search**.

2 Tap **Settings**.

3 Type **uninstall**.

Windows 8 displays the "uninstall" search results.

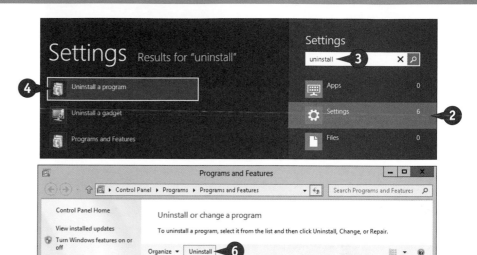

4 Tap **Uninstall a program**.

The Programs and Features window appears.

5 Tap the app that you want to uninstall.

6 Tap **Uninstall** (or **Uninstall/Change**).

In most cases, the app asks you to confirm that you want to uninstall the app.

7 Tap **Yes**.

The app's uninstall procedure begins.

8 Follow the instructions on the screen, which vary from app to app.

TIPS

What is the difference between an Automatic and a Custom uninstall?

Some apps give you a choice of uninstall procedures. The Automatic uninstall requires no input from you. It is the easiest, safest choice and therefore the one you should choose. The Custom uninstall gives you more control but is more complex and thus suitable only for experienced users.

If I uninstall an app, will I lose any documents or other files that I created with the app?

No. Uninstalling an app removes only the files used by the app itself and deletes any settings the app may have added to Windows. Any documents or files that you created with the app remain in your user account libraries.

CHAPTER 3

Customizing Windows 8

Windows 8 comes with a number of features that enable you to personalize your computer. Not only can you change the appearance of Windows 8 to suit your taste, but you can also change the way Windows 8 works to make it easier to use and more efficient.

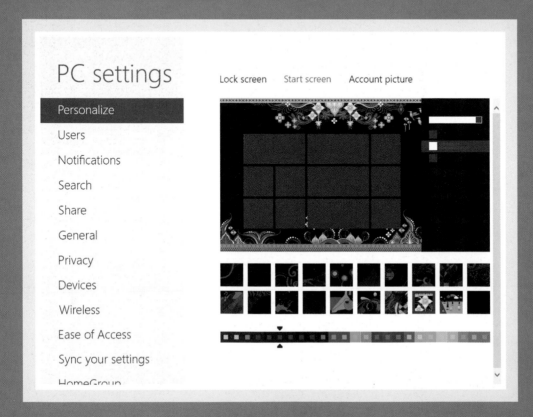

Configure the Start Screen

You can personalize how the Start screen looks and operates to suit your style and the way you work. For example, you can rearrange the Start screen tiles so that the apps you use most often appear together on the screen.

You can also make your Start screen more useful or more efficient by resizing some of the app screen tiles. The Start screen supports two sizes of app tiles: small and large. They are both the same height, but the larger size is twice as wide.

Configure the Start Screen

Move a Tile

1 On the Windows 8 Start screen, tap and hold the app tile that you want to move.

2 Drag the tile to the position that you prefer.

A Windows 8 reduces the tile sizes slightly and adds extra space between the tiles.

3 Release the tile.

B Windows 8 moves the tile to the new position.

Change a Tile Size

1 Swipe down on the app tile that you want to resize.

C Windows 8 displays the application bar.

2 Tap **Smaller**.

Note: If the tile is small and you want to enlarge it, tap **Larger** instead.

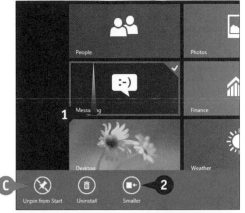

D Windows 8 resizes the tile.

Can I combine similar apps into a single group of tiles?

Yes. For example, you might want to break out all the game-related apps into their own group. To create a group, drag the first app tile all the way to left edge of the screen until you see a vertical bar and then release the tile. Windows 8 creates a new group for the app tile. To add other tiles to the new group, drag and drop the tiles within the group.

Can I name an app group?

Yes. This is a good idea because it makes the Start screen even easier to use and navigate. To name a group, pinch the screen to zoom out of the Start screen. Swipe down on any tile in the group, tap **Name group**, type the group name, and then tap **Name**. Tap the screen to zoom back in to the Start screen.

Pin an App to the Start Screen

You can customize the Start screen to give yourself quick access to the programs that you use most often. If you have an app that does not appear on the Start menu, you usually open the app by swiping up from the bottom edge of the screen to reveal the application bar and then tapping **All Apps**. For the apps you use most often, you can avoid this extra work by *pinning* their icons permanently to the main Start screen.

After you have pinned an app to your Start screen, you can launch it by scrolling right and tapping the app.

Pin an App to the Start Screen

1 Swipe up from the bottom edge of the screen.

A The application bar appears.

2 Tap **All apps**.

The Apps screen appears.

3 Locate the app that you want to pin to the Start screen.

4 Swipe down on the app tile.

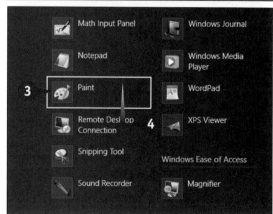

B The application bar appears.

5 Tap **Pin to Start**.

6 Swipe left from the right edge of the screen.

7 Tap **Start**.

Windows 8 returns to the Start screen.

8 Scroll to the right.

C A tile for the pinned app appears on the Start screen.

TIPS

Can I remove an app from the Start screen?

Yes, you can remove any app tile from the Start screen, even the default apps that come with Windows 8. To do so, swipe down on the app tile to open the application bar and then tap **Unpin from Start**.

What happens if the app I want to pin does not appear in the Apps screen?

If you do not see the app in the Apps screen, you can still pin the app to the Start screen by searching for it. Switch to the Start screen and begin typing the name of the app that you want to pin. Windows 8 switches to the Apps Search screen and begins displaying a list of apps with names that match your search text. Keep typing until you see the app. Tap and hold the app, drag it down slightly until it is selected, release it, and then tap **Pin to Start**.

Open the PC Settings App

You can configure and customize many aspects of your Windows 8 system using the PC Settings app.

PC Settings is the Windows 8 app that you use for customizing and tweaking your PC. Many of the tasks that follow in this chapter, including changing the Start and Lock screen backgrounds and adding an app to the Lock screen, are performed using the PC Settings app. PC Settings also offers a wealth of other options that you can use to customize your PC.

Open the PC Settings App

1 Swipe left from the right edge of the screen.

The Charms menu appears.

2 Tap **Settings**.

The Settings pane appears.

3 Tap **Change PC settings**.

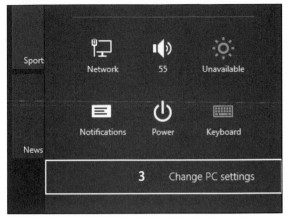

The PC Settings app appears.

A Use the tabs on the left side of the screen to navigate the PC Settings app.

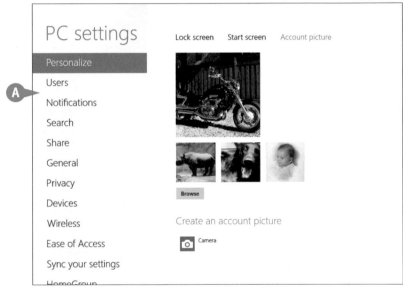

TIP

If I know which tab of the PC Settings app I want to use, is there a quick way to display it?
Yes, you can use the Settings Search pane, which enables you to quickly search for the setting that you want to work with. Swipe in from the right edge of the screen, tap **Search**, tap **Settings**, and then begin typing the name of the tab or setting you want. For example, if you want to go directly to the Users tab, type **users** and then tap **Users** in the search results.

49

Change the Start Screen Background

To give Windows 8 a different look, you can change the default Start screen background.

The Start screen background is the area that appears "behind" the tiles. By default, it consists of an abstract pattern formatted with a green color scheme. If you find yourself using the Start screen frequently, the default background might become tiresome. If so, you can liven things up a bit by changing both the background pattern and the background color.

Change the Start Screen Background

1 Open the PC Settings app.

Note: See the preceding section, "Open the PC Settings App."

2 Tap **Personalize**.

The Personalize tab appears.

3 Tap **Start screen**.

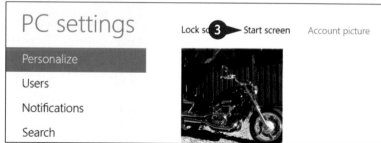

The Start Screen options appear.

4 Tap the background image that you want to use.

5 Tap the background color that you want to use.

The background image and color that you chose will now appear on your Start screen.

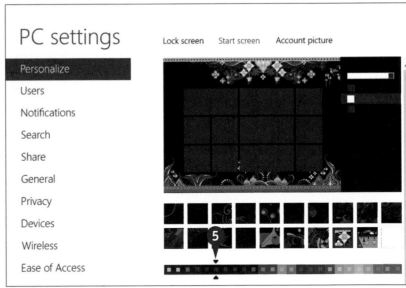

TIP

My eyesight is not what it used to be. Is there a way to make the Start screen more readable?

Windows 8 tends to use fairly subtle colors and small text, so the screen can be hard to read if your eyesight is poor. The solution is to switch to High Contrast mode, which uses white text on a black background. You can also increase the size of the screen elements.

To set this up, open the PC Settings app, tap the **Ease of Access** tab, tap the **High contrast** switch to **On**, and tap the **Make everything on your screen bigger** switch to **On**.

Change the Lock Screen Background

You can make your lock screen more interesting by changing the image that appears as its background.

As you learn in Chapter 13, "Implementing Security," locking your computer is a useful safety feature because it prevents unauthorized users from accessing your files and your network. If you find yourself looking at the lock screen frequently, you might prefer to see something other than the default image. Windows 8 comes with several system pictures that you can use, or you can use one of your own pictures.

Change the Lock Screen Background

Choose a System Picture

1 Open the PC Settings app.

Note: See the section "Open the PC Settings App" earlier in this chapter.

2 Tap **Personalize**.

3 Tap **Lock screen**.

The Lock Screen options appear.

4 Tap the picture that you want to use.

The image appears the next time that you lock your computer.

Choose One of Your Own Pictures

1 Open the PC Settings app.

Note: See the section "Open the PC Settings App" earlier in this chapter.

2 Tap **Personalize**.

3 Tap **Lock screen**.

The Lock Screen options appear.

4 Tap **Browse**.

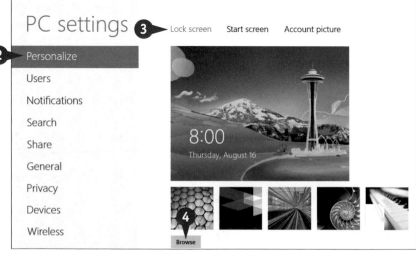

5 Tap **Files**.

6 Tap the folder that contains the picture you want to use.

7 If the picture resides in a subfolder, tap that subfolder to open it.

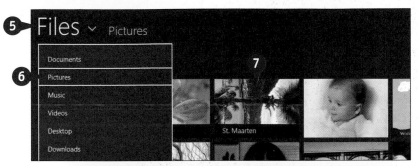

8 Tap the picture that you want to use.

9 Tap **Choose picture**.

The image appears the next time that you lock your computer.

TIP

Can I change the desktop background?

Yes. To do so, follow these steps:

1 Swipe from the right edge of the screen, tap **Search**, and then tap **Settings**.

2 Type **desktop** and then tap **Change desktop background**.

The Desktop Background window appears.

3 Tap the **Picture location** ⌄ and then tap the background gallery that you want to use.

4 Tap the image or color that you want to use.

5 Tap **Save changes**.

The picture or color that you selected appears on the desktop.

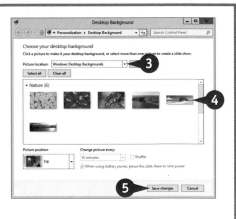

Add an App to the Lock Screen

When you lock your PC, Windows 8 displays icons for apps that have had recent notifications. For example, the Mail app shows the number of unread messages, and the Messages app shows the number of new text messages. The lock screen also shows any new notifications that appear for these apps.

If you lock your computer frequently, you can make the lock screen even more useful by adding icons for other apps, including ones that support notifications.

Add an App to the Lock Screen

1 Open the PC Settings app.

Note: See the section "Open the PC Settings App" earlier in this chapter.

2 Tap **Personalize**.

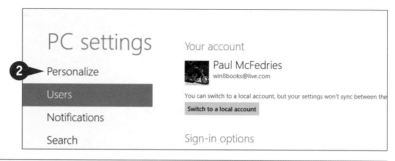

The Personalize tab appears.

3 Tap **Lock screen**.

The Lock Screen options appear.

4 Tap the Add button (⊕).

The Choose an App window appears.

5 Tap the app that you want to add to the lock screen.

6 To add an app to display a detailed status, tap ⊞.

7 Tap the app.

Windows 8 puts the new settings into effect, and the apps appear on the lock screen the next time that you use it.

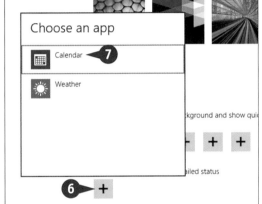

TIP

What is the difference between a quick status and detailed status?

A *quick status* means that the lock screen shows only a small icon for an app, and that icon displays the number of recent or unread items, such as the number of unread e-mail messages in the Mail app (A). A *detailed status* means that the lock screen shows more information from the app. For example, if you have an upcoming event in the Calendar app, the lock screen shows the details of that event, including the event title, location, and time (B).

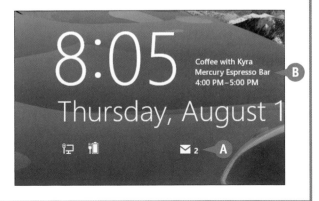

Synchronize Settings between PCs

If, besides your Windows 8 desktop computer, you also have a Windows 8 tablet, and a Windows 8 smartphone, using the same Microsoft account on each means that you can synchronize data among them. You can sync customizations, such as backgrounds and themes; system settings, such as languages and regional settings; Internet Explorer data, such as favorites and history; app settings; and more. This gives you a consistent interface across your devices and consistent data so that you can be more productive.

Synchronize Settings between PCs

① Open the PC Settings app.

Note: See the section "Open the PC Settings App" earlier in this chapter.

② Tap **Sync your settings**.

The Sync Your Settings screen appears.

③ Tap **Sync settings on this PC** to **On**.

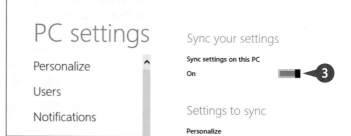

④ Under **Settings to Sync**, tap the switch to **Off** beside each type of setting that you do not want to include in the sync.

The next time Windows 8 syncs, it does not include the settings that your turned off.

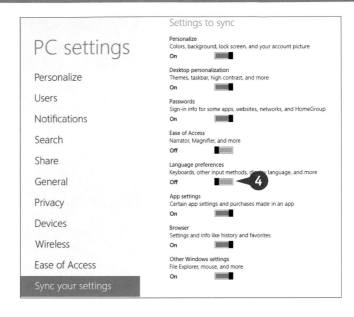

TIPS

Can I prevent syncing during those times when I am using a metered Internet connection that allows me only so much data?

By default, Windows 8 syncs with other PCs when you are using a metered Internet connection. To turn this off, follow steps **1** and **2** in this section to display the Sync Your Settings screen, scroll to the bottom, and then tap the **Sync settings over metered connections** switch to **Off**.

How does Windows 8 know when I am using a metered Internet connection?

You have to tell Windows 8 when you are using a metered connection. Swipe left from the right edge, tap **Settings**, tap the Network icon (▦), tap and hold your Internet connection, and then tap **Set as metered connection**.

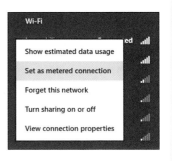

Access an App's Features

By design, Windows 8 apps appear simple and uncomplicated. They take up the entire screen, and when you first launch them, you usually see a fairly basic interface. However, almost all Windows 8 apps include a number of features — commands, settings, views, and so on — that you cannot see at first. To access these features, you must display the application bar — sometimes called the *app bar* — a strip that appears along the bottom or top of the screen. You can then tap the feature that you want to use.

Access an App's Features

Display the Application Bar

1 Open the Windows 8 app that you want to work with.

2 Swipe up from the bottom edge of the screen.

Ⓐ The application bar appears.

Ⓑ The application bar's icons represent the app's features.

Hide the Application Bar

Note: If you tap an application bar feature, the app automatically hides the application bar. You need to hide the application bar by hand only if you decide not to select a feature.

1 Tap an empty section of the app screen outside of the application bar.

C The app hides the application bar.

TIPS

Do Windows 8 apps always display a single application bar at the bottom of the screen?
No. In some apps, the application bar appears at the top of the screen, and in other apps, you see *two* application bars — one on the bottom and one on the top of the screen.

Are there more app features that I can access?
Yes, you can also display the Settings pane for each app. The layout of the Settings pane varies between apps, but it usually includes commands for setting app preferences and options. To display an app's Settings pane, swipe left from the right edge of the screen and then tap **Settings**.

Pin an App to the Taskbar

The earlier section "Pin an App to the Start Screen" covers pinning an app to the Start screen, but that is helpful only if you use the Start screen regularly. If you use the desktop more often and you have an app that you use frequently, you might prefer to have that app just a single tap away. You can achieve this by pinning the app to the taskbar.

You can pin an app to the taskbar either from the Start screen or from the desktop.

Pin an App to the Taskbar

Using the Start Screen

1 Swipe left from the right edge of the screen and then tap **Search**.

2 Type the name of the app that you want to pin to the taskbar.

Windows 8 displays the search results.

3 Swipe down on the app.

4 Tap **Pin to taskbar**.

Ⓐ An icon for the app now appears on the taskbar.

From the Desktop

① Launch the app that you want to pin to the taskbar.

② Tap and hold the running app's taskbar icon.

③ Tap **Pin this program to taskbar**.

④ Tap ❌.

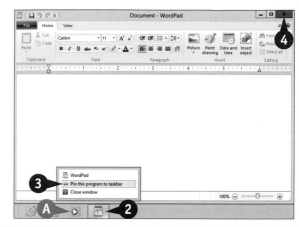

Ⓑ An icon for the app remains on the taskbar.

<hr/>

TIPS

Can I change the order of the taskbar icons?
Yes. As you drop app icons onto the taskbar, Windows 8 displays the icons left to right in the order that you added them. If you prefer a different order, tap and drag a taskbar icon to the left or right and then drop it in the new position. Note that this technique applies not only to the icons pinned to the taskbar, but also to the icons for any running programs.

How do I remove an app icon from the taskbar?
If you decide that you no longer require an app to be pinned to the taskbar, you should remove it to reduce taskbar clutter and provide more room for other app icons. To remove a pinned app icon, tap and hold the icon and then tap **Unpin this program from taskbar**.

Adjust the Volume

While an audio or video file is playing, you can adjust the volume up or down to get its audio just right.

If you are listening to media by yourself, you can adjust the volume to suit the music and your mood. However, if there are other people nearby, you will probably want to use the volume control to keep the playback volume low to avoid disturbing them. If you need to silence the media temporarily, you can mute the playback.

Adjust the Volume

1 Swipe left from the right edge of the screen and then tap **Settings**.

The Settings pane appears.

2 Tap the Volume icon (🔊).

3 Tap and drag the slider to set the volume level that you want.

A You can also tap 🔊 to mute the volume.

Windows 8 sets the system volume to the new level.

Set the Time Zone

To ensure that your system clock is accurate, you should set the time zone to correspond to your location.

When Windows 8 configures your computer, it performs a number of chores, including setting the current system time and time zone. However, for the time zone, Windows 8 defaults to Pacific time in North America. If this is not the time zone used where you live, you must select the correct one to ensure that you have the accurate system time.

Set the Time Zone

1 Open the PC Settings app.

Note: See the section "Open the PC Settings App" earlier in this chapter.

2 Tap **General**.

3 Tap the **Time** ⌄.

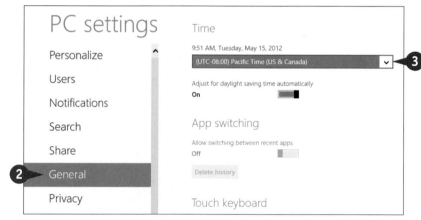

4 Tap your time zone.

Windows 8 adjusts the time to the new time zone.

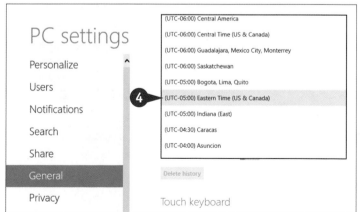

CHAPTER 4

Surfing the Web

This chapter discusses the web and shows you how to use Internet Explorer to navigate from site to site. You also learn how to select links, enter web page addresses, work with tabs, save your favorite sites, search for information, and more.

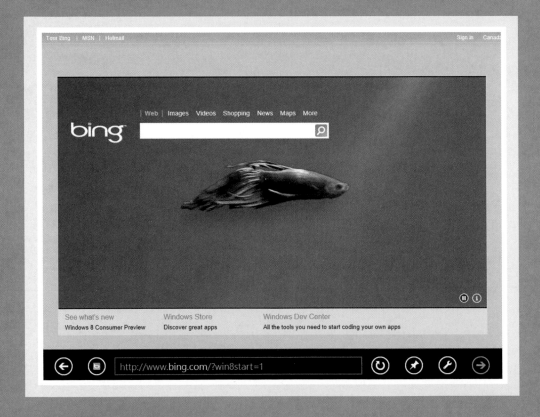

Understanding the World Wide Web

The *World Wide Web* — the *web,* for short — is a massive storehouse of information that resides on computers called *web servers,* located all over the world. You will probably find that you spend the majority of your online time browsing the web. That is not surprising because the web is useful, entertaining, fun, interesting, and provocative.

This section introduces you to the web. In particular, you learn about four crucial web concepts: web pages, websites, web addresses, and links. Understanding these ideas can help you get the most out of your web excursions.

Web Pages

World Wide Web information is presented on *web pages,* which you download to your tablet using a web browser program, such as Windows 8's Internet Explorer. Each web page can combine text with images, sounds, music, and even video to present you with information on a particular subject. The web consists of billions of pages covering almost every imaginable topic.

Websites

A *website* is a collection of web pages associated with a particular person, business, service, government, school, or organization. Websites are stored on a *web server,* a special computer that makes web pages available for people to browse. A web server is usually a powerful computer capable of handling thousands of site visitors at a time. The largest websites are run by *server farms,* which are networks that may contain dozens, hundreds, or even thousands of servers.

Web Addresses

Every web page has its own *web address* that uniquely identifies the page. This address is sometimes called a *URL* (pronounced *yoo-ar-ell* or *erl*), which is short for *Uniform Resource Locator.* If you know the address of a page, you can plug that address into your web browser to view the page.

http://www.wordspy.com/

Links

A *link* (also called a *hyperlink*) is a kind of cross-reference to another web page. Each link is a bit of text — usually shown underlined and in a different color — or an image that, when you tap it, loads the other page into your web browser automatically. The other page is often from the same site, but links that take you to pages anywhere on the web are also common.

Tickling your buying bone
BUY IT ONLINE
Amazon.com
Amazon.ca
Amazon.co.uk
Barnes & Noble.com
Indigo (Canada)

Start Internet Explorer

To access websites and view web pages, you must use a web browser program. In Windows 8, the default web browser is Internet Explorer, which you can use to surf websites when your tablet is connected to the Internet.

The desktop version of Internet Explorer offers a number of features that make it easy to browse the web. For example, you can open multiple pages in a single window, save your favorite sites for easier access, and perform Internet searches from the Internet Explorer window.

Start Internet Explorer

1 On the Start screen, tap **Internet Explorer**.

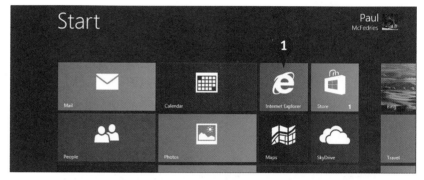

The Internet Explorer window appears.

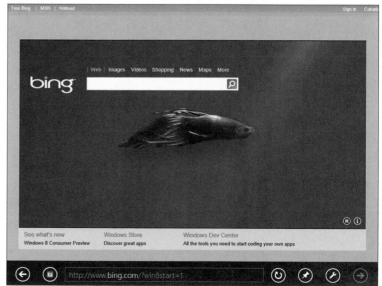

Navigate Internet Explorer

You can easily surf the web if you know your way around the Internet Explorer web browser. In particular, you need to familiarize yourself with important Internet Explorer features such as the address bar and where the program displays the web page title. You also need to understand links, how to recognize the current link, and how to determine where a link will take you before tapping it.

Ⓐ Web Page Title

This part of Internet Explorer shows the title of the displayed web page. Note that you see this only when you swipe down from the top edge of the screen.

Ⓑ Links

Links appear as either text or images. On most pages, although not the page shown here, text links appear underlined and in a different color — usually blue — than the regular page text.

Ⓒ Current Link

This is the link that you are currently pointing to with your stylus. The stylus pointer changes to 🖑. On some pages, such as this one, the link text also becomes underlined.

Ⓓ Address Bar

This text box displays the address of the displayed web page. You can also use the address bar to type the address of a web page that you want to visit to search for information on the web. You see this only when you swipe down from the top edge of the screen or swipe up from the bottom.

Ⓔ Link Address

When you point at a link, Internet Explorer displays a tooltip that shows you the address of the page associated with the link.

Select a Link

Almost all web pages include links to pages that contain related information. When you select a link, your browser loads the other page.

Links come in two forms: text and images. Text links consist of a word or phrase that usually appears underlined and in a different color from the normal page text. However, web designers can control the look of their links, so text links may not always stand out like this. The only way to tell is to position the stylus pointer over the text or image; if the pointer changes to 🖑, the item is a link.

Select a Link

1 Position the stylus pointer over the link (the pointer changes to 🖑).

A This tooltip shows the address of the linked page.

2 Tap the text or image.

Note: The link address shown when you point at a link may be different than the one shown when the page is downloading. This happens when the website redirects the link, which happens frequently.

The linked web page appears.

B The web page address changes after the linked page is loaded.

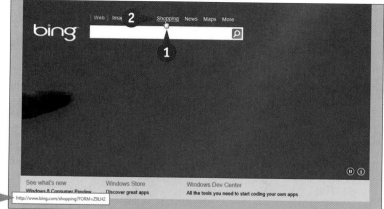

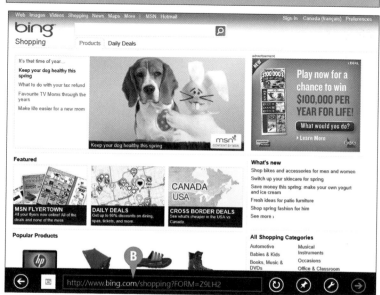

Enter a Web Page Address

If you know the address of a specific web page, you can type it into the web browser to display it. Every web page is uniquely identified by an address called the *Uniform Resource Locator,* or *URL.* The URL is composed of four basic parts: the transfer method (usually http, which stands for *Hypertext Transfer Protocol*), the website domain name, the directory where the web page is located on the server, and the web page filename.

The website domain name suffix most often used is .com (commercial), but other common suffixes include .gov (government), .org (nonprofit organization), .edu (education), and country domains such as .ca (Canada).

Enter a Web Page Address

1 Tap in the address bar.

Note: If you do not see the address bar, swipe up from the bottom edge of the screen.

Internet Explorer displays a list of the pages that you have visited most frequently.

A If you see the page that you want, tap it and skip the rest of these steps.

2 Tap ⌫.

Internet Explorer clears the address bar.

Note: Step 2 is optional.

3 Type the address of the web page.

B If the address uses the .com suffix, you can add it quickly by tapping the **.com** key.

4 Tap the Go button (⊙).

C You can also tap the **Go** key.

D A tile appears here if you have previously visited the page, so you can also tap the tile to load the page.

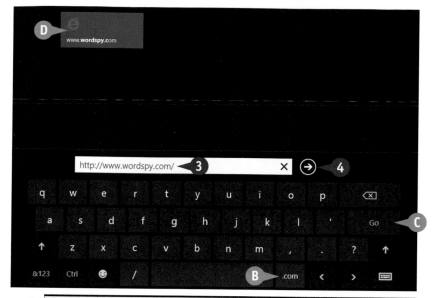

The web page appears.

TIP

Are there any shortcuts that I can use to enter web page addresses?

Here are a couple useful keyboard techniques:

- Most web addresses begin with *http://*. You can leave off these characters when you type your address; Internet Explorer adds them automatically.

- If the address uses the form `http://www.something.com`, type just the `something` part, tap the **Ctrl** key, and then tap the **Go** key. Internet Explorer automatically adds *http://www.* at the beginning and *.com* at the end.

Open a Web Page in a Tab

As you surf the web, you may come upon a page that you want to keep available while you visit other sites. That page may contain important information that you need to reference, or it might be a page that you want to read later on.

Instead of leaving the page and trying to find it again later, Internet Explorer lets you keep the page open in a special section of the browser screen called a *tab*. You can use a second tab to visit your other sites and then resume viewing the first site by tapping its tab.

Open a Web Page in a Tab

Open a Web Page in a Tab

1 Swipe down from the top edge of the screen.

A The tab bar appears.

2 Tap the New Tab button (⊕).

Internet Explorer prompts you for the web page address.

3 Follow the steps in the "Enter a Web Page Address" section to display the page.

Open a Link in a Tab

1 Tap and hold the link that you want to open.

B Internet Explorer displays a list of actions for the link.

2 Tap **Open link in new tab**.

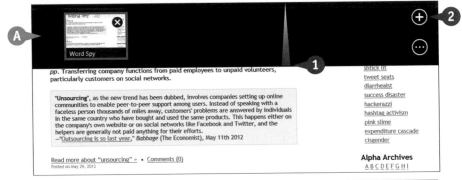

Internet Explorer loads the page in a new tab.

3 Swipe down from the top edge of the screen.

C The tab bar appears.

4 Tap the tab.

The web page loaded in the tab appears.

Work with Tabs

1 Swipe down from the top edge of the screen.

D The tab bar appears.

E Tap a tab to switch to that page.

F Tap ⊗ to close a tab.

TIP

Is there an easy way to close all my tabs except the one that I am currently using?

Yes, you can do so by following these steps:

1 Switch to the tab that you want to leave open.

2 Swipe down from the top of the screen.

The tab bar appears.

3 Tap the More button (⊙).

4 Tap **Close tabs**.

Internet Explorer closes all the tabs except the current one.

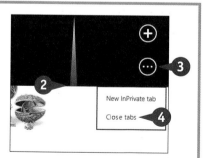

Navigate Web Pages

After you have visited several pages, you can return to a page that you visited earlier. Instead of retyping the address or looking for the link, Internet Explorer gives you some easier methods.

When you navigate from page to page, you create a kind of "path" through the web. Internet Explorer keeps track of this path by maintaining a list of the pages that you have visited. You can use that list to go back to a page. After you have gone back, you can also use that same list to go forward through the pages again.

Navigate Web Pages

Go Back One Page

1 Swipe up from the bottom of the screen.

The address bar appears.

2 Tap the Back button (⬅).

The previous page that you visited appears.

Go Forward One Page

1 Swipe up from the bottom of the screen.

The address bar appears.

2 Tap the Forward button (➡).

The next page that you visited appears.

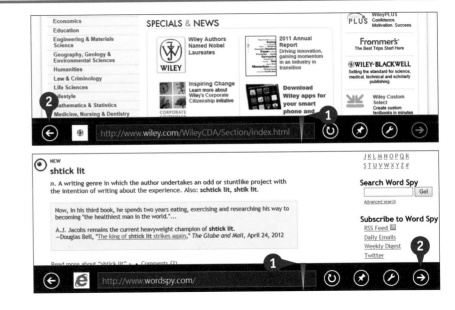

Find Text on a Page

When you are reading a page on the web, it is not unusual to be looking for specific information. In those situations, rather than read through the entire page to find the information that you are looking for, you can search the web page text for the data. Internet Explorer's Find on Page feature lets you to do that by enabling you to search through the current page text for a specific word or phrase.

Find Text on a Page

1 Swipe up from the bottom of the screen.

The address bar appears.

2 Tap the Tools button (⌀).

3 Tap **Find on page**.

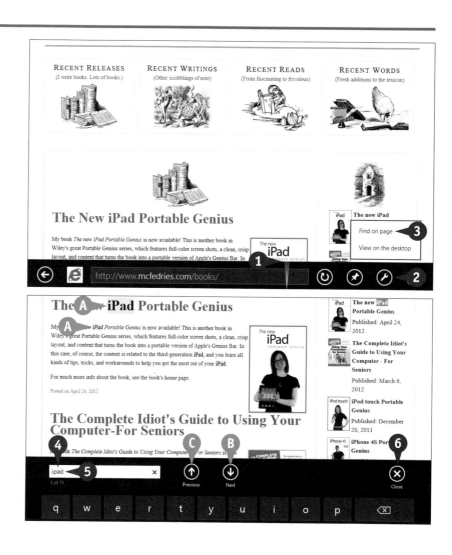

The Find on Page bar appears.

4 Tap inside the text box.

5 Type the word or phrase that you want to locate.

Ⓐ Internet Explorer highlights the matching text on the page.

Ⓑ Tap **Next** to cycle forward through the matches.

Ⓒ Tap **Previous** to cycle backward through the matches.

6 When you are done, tap **Close**.

Save Favorite Web Pages

If you have web pages that you visit frequently, you can save yourself time by saving those pages as favorites within Internet Explorer. This enables you to display the pages with just a couple taps.

You save favorite pages in Internet Explorer by *pinning* them. This adds the pages to the Pinned list within Internet Explorer. Instead of typing an address or searching for one of these pages, you can display the web page by tapping it in the Pinned list.

Save Favorite Web Pages

Save a Favorite Web Page

1 Display the web page that you want to save.

2 Swipe up from the bottom of the screen.

The address bar appears.

3 Tap the Pin Site button (⊚).

4 Tap **Pin to Start**.

The Pin to Start options appear.

5 Edit the page name, as necessary.

6 Tap **Pin to Start**.

Internet Explorer adds the page to the Pinned list.

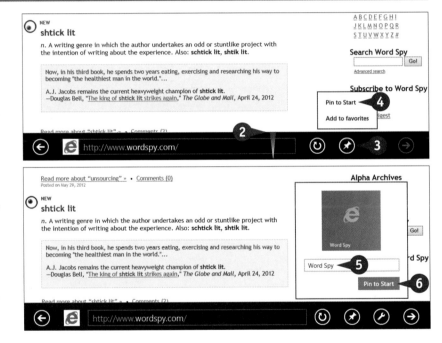

Display a Favorite Web Page

1 Swipe up from the bottom of the screen.

The address bar appears.

2 Tap inside the address box.

3 Slide the screen left.

A The Pinned list appears.

4 Tap the web page that you want to display.

The web page appears.

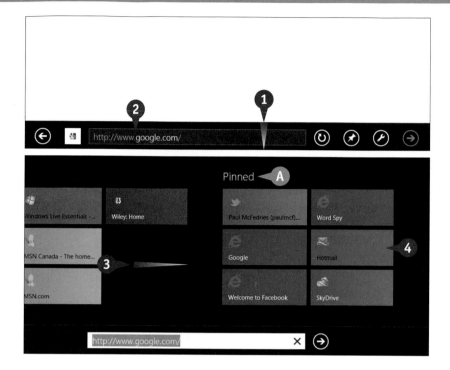

TIPS

Why is the button named "Pin to Start"?
That is because not only does Internet Explorer add a pinned page to the Pinned list within the program, but it also creates a tile for the pinned page on the Start screen. This means that you can display a pinned page by tapping its Start screen tile.

How do I delete a favorite?
Display the Start screen, swipe down on the tile of the pinned page that you want to delete, and then tap **Unpin from Start**.

Search for Sites

If you need information on a specific topic, Internet Explorer has a built-in feature that enables you to quickly search the web for sites that have the information you require.

The web has a number of sites called *search engines* that enable you to find what you are looking for. By default, Internet Explorer uses the Bing search site. You use Internet Explorer's address bar to enter a word or phrase that is representative of the information that you seek. Internet Explorer passes the word or phrase to Bing, which then looks for pages that match your text.

Search for Sites

1 Tap inside the address bar.

Note: If you do not see the address bar, swipe up from the bottom edge of the screen.

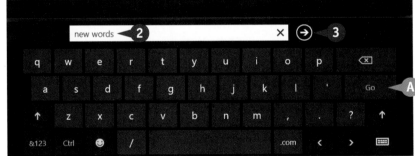

2 Type a word, phrase, or question that represents the information that you want to find.

3 Tap ➡.

Ⓐ You can also tap the **Go** key.

B A list of pages that match your search text appears.

4 Tap a web page.

The page appears.

CHAPTER 5

Sending E-mail and Messages

You can use the Mail app to send e-mail messages, as well as to receive and read incoming messages. You can use the Messaging app to send and respond to instant messages.

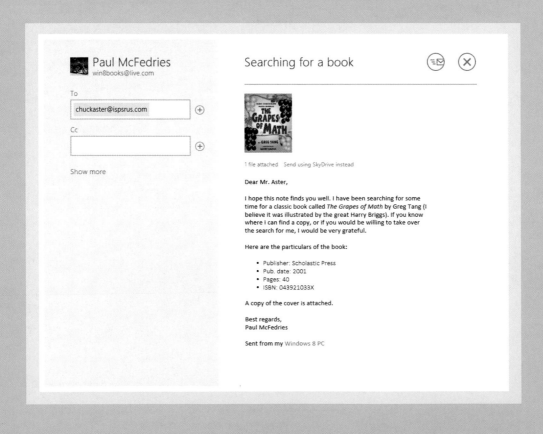

Configure an E-mail Account

Before you can send an e-mail message, you must add your e-mail account to the Mail application. This also enables you to use Mail to retrieve the messages that others have sent to your account.

You use Mail to set up web-based e-mail accounts with services such as Hotmail and Gmail. Note, however, that if you are already signing in to Windows 8 using a Microsoft account, then Windows 8 automatically adds that account to the Mail app — so you need to follow the steps in this section only if you want to add another account to Mail.

Configure an E-mail Account

Configure an Initial E-mail Account

1 On the Start screen, tap **Mail**.

If you are not signed in with a Microsoft account, Mail asks for your account e-mail address and password.

2 Type your e-mail address.

3 Type your e-mail password.

4 Tap **Sign in**.

The Mail app signs you in to your account.

Configure Another E-mail Account

1 In Mail, swipe from the right edge of the screen.

The Charms menu appears.

2 Tap **Settings**.

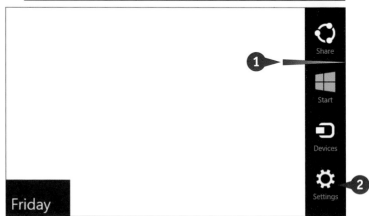

The Settings menu appears.

3 Tap **Accounts**.

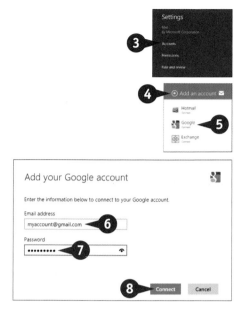

The Accounts pane appears.

4 Tap **Add an account**.

The Add an Account menu appears.

5 Tap the type of account that you want to add.

Mail asks for your account e-mail address and password.

6 Type your e-mail address.

7 Type your e-mail password.

8 Tap **Connect**.

Mail add your e-mail account to the Accounts pane.

TIP

How do I add my Exchange account to Mail?

You will need to obtain from your Exchange administrator or provider the account's server address, domain name, and username — and you will need to know your account's e-mail address and password, of course. In many cases, you can follow steps **1** to **7** in the subsection "Configure Another E-mail Account" and then tap **See more**. You use the extra text boxes to enter the server address, domain, and username and then tap **Connect**.

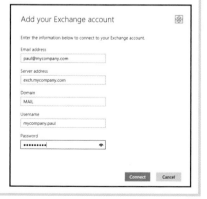

Send an E-mail Message

If you know the e-mail address of a person or organization, you can send an e-mail message to that address. Each address uniquely identifies the location of an Internet mailbox. An address takes the form *username@domain*, where *username* is the name of the person's account, and *domain* is the Internet name of the company that provides the person's e-mail account.

When you send an e-mail message, it travels through your ISP's outgoing mail server. This server routes the messages to the recipient's incoming mail server, which then stores the message in the recipient's mailbox.

Send an E-mail Message

1 In Mail, tap the New button (⊕).

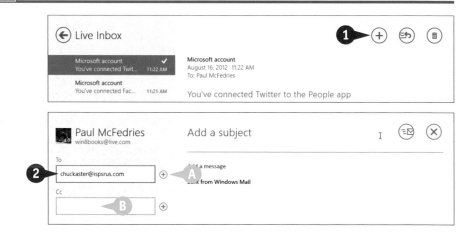

A message window appears.

2 Type the e-mail address of the recipient.

Note: You can add multiple e-mail addresses to the **To** line. Tap **Enter** after each address.

A To add someone from your contacts list, tap the Add button (⊕).

B To send a copy of the message to another person, type that person's e-mail address in the **Cc** field.

3 Type a subject for the message.

4 Type the message.

Note: See the following section, "Format the Message Text," to learn how to apply formatting to your message.

5 Tap the Send button ( ).

Mail sends your message.

TIP

Can I send a copy to someone but not let the other recipients see that person's address?

Yes, this is known as a *blind carbon copy* (Bcc, sometimes also called a *blind courtesy copy*). To include a blind carbon copy with your message, tap **Show more** to add the Bcc field and then use that field to type the person's address.

Format the Message Text

You can add visual interest and make your message easier to read by formatting your message text.

A plain e-mail message is quick to compose, but it is often worth the extra time to add formatting to your text. For example, you can add bold or italic formatting to highlight a word or phrase. Mail supports a wide range of formatting options, including font colors, highlights, emoticons, bulleted lists, and numbered lists. All of these formatting options have their place, but be careful not to overdo it, or you may make your message *harder* to read.

Format the Message Text

1. Select the text that you want to format.

2. Swipe down from the top of the screen.

3. Tap the formatting that you want to apply to the text.

   Mail applies the formatting to the text.

4. To add a list, tap where you want the list to appear.

5. Swipe down from the top of the screen.

6. Tap **More**.

7. Tap the type of list that you want to insert.

   Mail adds the bullet or number for the first item in the list.

Note: To complete the list, type each item and then tap Enter. When you are done, tap Enter twice.

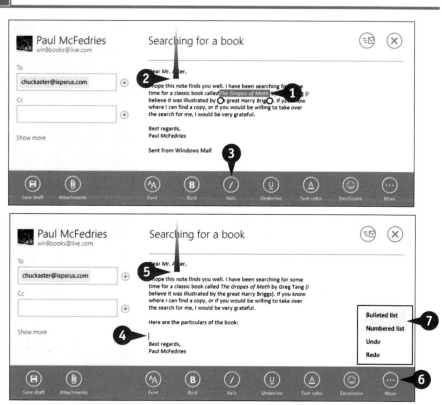

Set the Message Priority

You can set the priority level of your outgoing message to let the recipient know whether to handle your message with a high or low priority.

If you are sending a message that has important information or that requires a fast response, set the message's priority to high. When the recipient receives the message, his or her e-mail program indicates the high priority. Alternatively, you can set the priority to low for unimportant messages so that the recipient knows not to handle the message immediately.

Set the Message Priority

① Tap **Show more**.

② In the **Priority** list, tap the priority that you want to use.

Add a File Attachment

If you have a document that you want to send to another person, you can attach the document to an e-mail message. A typical e-mail message is fine for short notes, but you may have something more complex to communicate, such as budget numbers or a slide show, or some form of media that you want to share, such as an image or a song.

Because these more complex types of data usually come in a separate file — such as a spreadsheet, presentation file, or picture file — it makes sense to send that file to your recipient as an attachment.

Add a File Attachment

1 Swipe up from the bottom of the screen.

2 Tap **Attachments**.

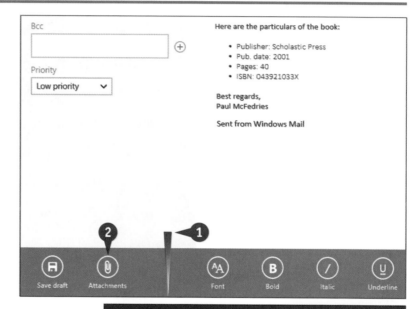

The Files screen appears.

3 Tap **Files**.

4 Tap the folder that contains the file you want to attach.

⑤ Tap the file that you want to attach.

⑥ Tap **Attach**.

Ⓐ Mail attaches the file to the message.

TIP

Is there a limit to the number of files that I can attach to a message?

There is no practical limit to the number of files that you can attach to a message. However, you should be careful with the total *size* of the files that you send. If you or the recipient has a slow Internet connection, sending or receiving the message can take an extremely long time. Also, many Internet service providers (ISPs) place a limit on the size of a message's attachments, which is usually between 2MB and 10MB. In general, use e-mail to send only a few small files at a time.

Save a Draft of a Message

If you cannot complete or send your message right away, you can save it as a draft and open it again later.

As you work on an e-mail message, you might find that you need to give it more thought or that you have to do more research. Rather than discard your work, you can close the message and have Mail save it for you. Mail stores the saved message in your account's Drafts folder. When you are ready to resume editing the message, you can open it from the Drafts folder.

Save a Draft of a Message

Save the Draft

1 Tap the Close button (⊗).

2 Tap **Save draft**.

Mail saves the message to your Drafts folder.

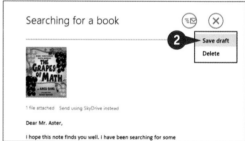

Open the Draft

1 Tap the Back button (⊙).

Mail displays your account folders.

2 Tap **Drafts**.

3 Tap the draft that you want to open.

4 Tap the Edit button (⊘).

Mail opens the message for editing.

What are the account folders used for?

Inbox	Holds incoming messages sent to you by other people.
Drafts	Holds outgoing messages that you have not yet sent.
Sent Items	Holds copies of outgoing messages that you have sent.
Outbox	Holds outgoing messages that are in the process of being sent.
Junk	Holds incoming messages that Mail has deemed to be unsolicited commercial e-mails, also known as *junk mail* or *spam*.
Deleted Items	Holds messages that you have deleted from other folders.

Receive and Read E-mail Messages

When another person sends you an e-mail message, that message ends up in your e-mail account's mailbox on the incoming mail server maintained by your ISP or e-mail provider. However, that company does not automatically pass along that message to you. Instead, you must use Mail to connect to your mailbox on the incoming mail server and then retrieve any messages waiting for you.

By default, Mail automatically checks for new messages every ten minutes while you are online, but you can also check for new messages at any time.

Receive and Read E-mail Messages

Receive E-mail Messages

1 Swipe up from the bottom edge of the screen.

A The application bar appears.

2 Tap **Sync**.

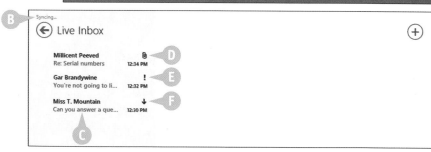

B Mail displays "Syncing..." as it checks for new messages.

C If you have new messages, they appear in your Inbox folder in bold type.

D The ⓤ symbol means that the message has an attachment.

E The ! symbol means that the message was sent with a high priority.

F The ↓ symbol means that the message was sent with a low priority.

92

Read a Message

1 Tap the message.

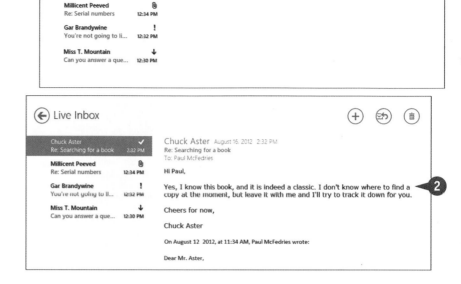

The message text appears in the preview pane.

2 Read the message text.

Why do new messages sometimes appear in my Inbox when I have not tapped the Sync button?
For certain types of accounts, Mail supports a feature called *push* that can send new messages to your Inbox automatically. In this case, when the mail server receives a new message, it immediately sends the message to your Inbox without your having to run the Sync command. Note that this feature works only if you are using a Hotmail or Windows Live e-mail account.

Reply to a Message

When a message you receive requires some kind of response — whether it is answering a question, supplying information, or providing comments — you can reply to that message.

Most replies go only to the person who sent the original message. However, you can also send the reply to all the people who were included in the original message's To and Cc lines. Mail includes the text of the original message in the reply, but you might want to edit the original message text to include only enough of the original message to put your reply into context.

Reply to a Message

1 Tap the message to which you want to reply.

2 Tap the Respond button (⊜).

3 Tap the reply type that you want to use.

Note: See the first Tip for more information.

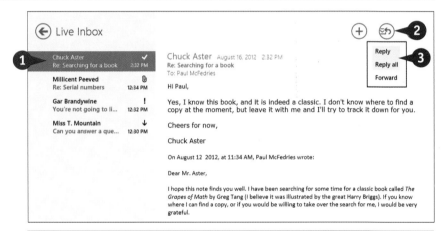

A message window appears.

Ⓐ Mail automatically inserts the sender of the original message as the recipient.

Ⓑ Mail also inserts the subject line, preceded by "RE:."

Ⓒ Mail includes the original message's addresses (To and From), date, subject, and text at the bottom of the reply.

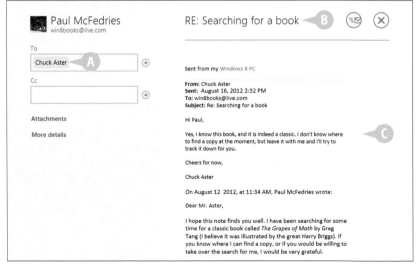

④ Edit the original message to include only the text relevant to your reply.

⑤ Tap the area above the original message text.

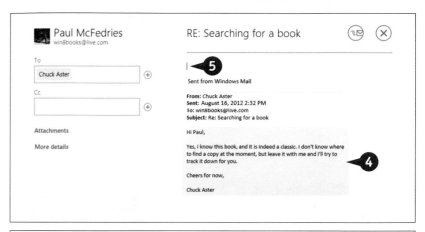

⑥ Type your reply.

⑦ Tap ⬚.

Mail sends your reply.

Note: Mail stores a copy of your reply in the Sent Items folder.

What is the difference between Reply and Reply All?

These commands determine who gets a copy of your reply:

• Tap **Reply** to respond only to the first address displayed on the To line.

• Tap **Reply all** to respond to all the addresses in the To and Cc lines.

Do I have to edit the original message text when I am composing my reply?

If the original message is fairly short, you usually do not need to edit the text. However, if the original message is long, and your response deals only with part of that message, you will save the recipient time by deleting everything except the relevant portion of the text.

Forward a Message

If a message has information that is relevant to or concerns another person, you can forward a copy of the message to that person. You can also include your own comments in the forward.

In the body of the forward, Mail includes the original message's addresses, date, and subject line. Below this information, Mail also includes the text of the original message. In most cases, you will leave the entire message intact so that your recipient can see it. However, if only part of the message is relevant to the recipient, you should edit the original message accordingly.

Forward a Message

1 Tap the message that you want to forward.

2 Tap 🔁.

3 Tap **Forward**.

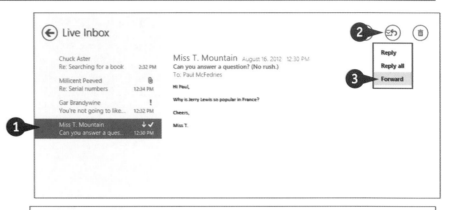

A message window appears.

Ⓐ Mail inserts the subject line, preceded by "FW:."

Ⓑ The original message's addresses (To and From), date, subject, and text are included at the bottom of the forward.

4 Select or type the e-mail address of the person to whom you are forwarding the message.

Ⓒ To send a copy of the message to another person, select or type that person's e-mail address in the **Cc** field.

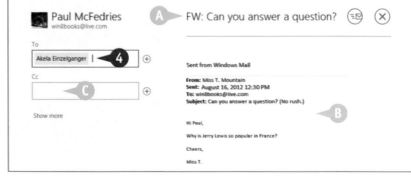

5 If necessary, edit the original message to include only the text relevant to your forward.

6 Tap the area above the original message text.

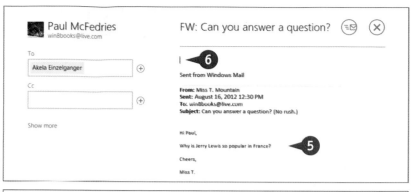

7 Type your comments.

8 Tap ✉.

Mail sends your forward.

Note: Mail stores a copy of your forward in the Sent Items folder.

TIP

Why does Mail sometimes set the priority of a forward or reply?
Mail forwards or replies to a message using the same priority as the original. This is rarely useful, so in most cases, you will want to set the priority to Normal before sending the forward or reply. To do this, tap **Show more**, tap the **Priority** ⌄, and then tap **Normal priority**.

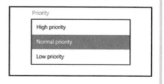

Open and Save an Attachment

When a message comes in and displays the attachment symbol (🖉), it means that the sender has included a file as an attachment to the message. If you just want to take a quick look at the file, you can open the attachment directly from Mail. Alternatively, if you want to keep a copy of the file on your computer, you can save the attachment to your hard drive.

Be careful when dealing with attached files. Computer viruses are often transmitted by e-mail attachments.

Open and Save an Attachment

Open an Attachment

1 Tap the message that has the attachment, as indicated by 🖉.

A A list of the message attachments appears.

2 Tap the attachment that you want to open.

Mail asks you to confirm that you want to open the file.

3 Tap **Open**.

The file opens in the appropriate program.

Note: Instead of opening the file, you may see a message that says, "Windows can't open this type of file." This means that you need to install the appropriate program for the type of file. If you are not sure, ask the person who sent you the file what program you need.

98

Save an Attachment

1 Tap the message that has the attachment, as indicated by 📎.

Ⓐ A list of the message attachments appears.

2 Tap the attachment that you want to save.

3 Tap **Save**.

The Files screen appears.

4 Tap **Files**.

5 Tap the folder that you want to use to store the file.

6 Edit the filename, if needed.

7 Tap **Save**.

Mail saves the attachment to your tablet's hard drive.

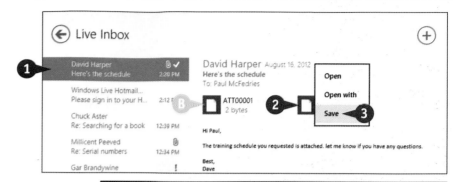

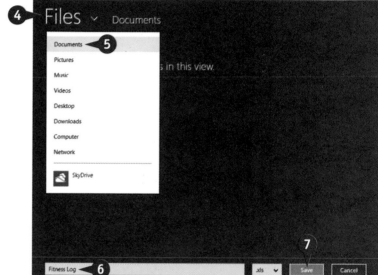

Can I open an attachment using some other program than the one Mail chooses?

Yes. When you tap **Open**, Mail automatically opens the file in the app associated with that type of file. For example, text files open in the Notepad app. However, you can tell Mail to open the file using a different app, if you prefer. Tap the message that contains the attachment, tap the attachment that you want to open, and then tap **Open with**. Mail displays a list of apps that you can use to open the file. Tap the app that you want to use. If you do not see the app that you want, tap **More options** to expand the list.

Delete a Message

After you have used Mail for a while, you may find that you have many messages in your Inbox folder. The more messages you have, the harder it becomes to find a message that you want and the more time-consuming it gets to navigate the messages. To keep the Inbox uncluttered and easier to navigate, you should delete any messages that you have already read and do not need to keep.

Note that when you delete a message, Mail actually just sends it to the Deleted Items folder. If you delete a message accidentally, you can retrieve it from Deleted Items.

Delete a Message

Delete a Message from the Inbox

1 Tap the message that you want to delete.

2 Tap the Delete button (🗑).

Mail removes the message from the Inbox and moves it to the Deleted Items folder.

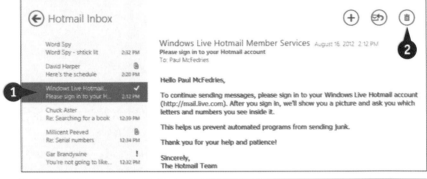

Restore a Deleted Message

1 Tap ⬅.

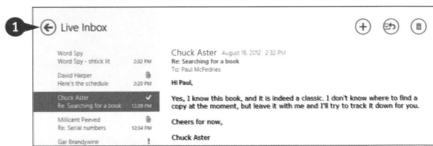

Mail displays the folders list.

2 Tap **Deleted items**.

Mail opens the Deleted Items folder.

3 Tap the message that you want to restore.

4 Swipe up from the bottom of the screen.

Ⓐ The application bar appears.

5 Tap **Move**.

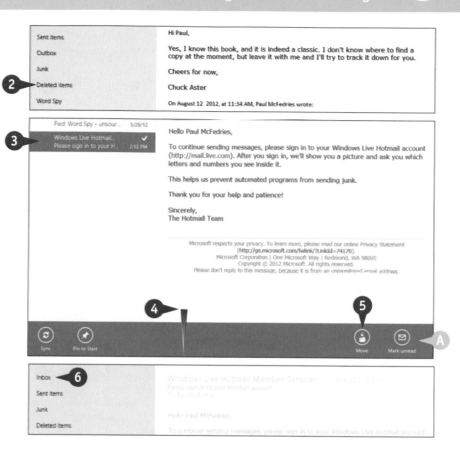

Mail displays the folders list again.

6 Tap **Inbox**.

Mail restores the message to the Inbox folder.

Can I move a message to a folder that I have created, instead of to the Inbox?

Yes, but you must first access your Microsoft account on the web to create the folder. Follow these steps:

1 Open Internet Explorer and go to http://mail.live.com.

2 Sign in to your account.

3 In the Folders list, tap **New folder**.

4 Type the name of the new folder and then tap `Enter`.

5 Return to the Mail app.

6 Swipe up from the bottom of the screen and then tap **Sync**.

Mail adds the new folder to the folders list.

7 Tap the message that you want to move.

8 Swipe up from the bottom of the screen and then tap **Move**.

9 Tap the new folder.

Mail moves the message to that folder.

Send an Instant Message

Windows 8 includes the Messaging app to enable you to exchange instant messages with other people who are online.

An instant messaging conversation begins by one person inviting another person to exchange messages. In Messaging, this means sending an initial instant message. You can send an instant message to your Microsoft account contacts and to your Facebook friends, as long as they are online and are accepting instant messages. See Chapter 6, "Getting Social with Your Tablet," to learn how to connect your Facebook account to your Microsoft account.

Send an Instant Message

1 On the Start screen, tap **Messaging**.

The Messaging app appears.

2 Tap **New message**.

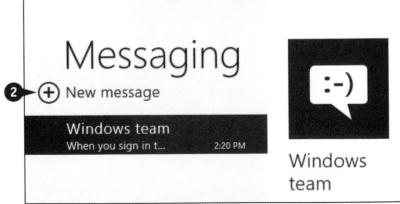

The People app appears.

3 Tap **Online only**.

4 Tap the person to whom you want to send a message.

5 Tap **Select**.

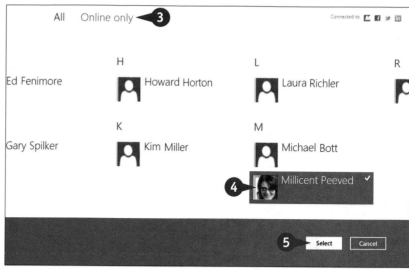

Messaging opens a new instant messaging conversation.

6 Type your message.

7 Tap Enter.

Messaging sends the message.

A Your messages and the recipient's replies appear here.

Is there a quick way to resume a conversation with someone?

Yes, Windows 8 gives you a couple ways to resume a conversation quickly. First, note that the left side of the Messaging app displays a list of the people that you have had conversations with in the past. So to resume a conversation, open Messaging and then tap the person's name in the left pane.

Alternatively, you can pin a person to the Start screen. Open the People app, tap the person that you want to pin, swipe up from the bottom of the screen to open the application bar, tap **Pin to Start**, and then tap **Pin to Start** once again. To resume a conversation with that person, tap his or her tile on the Start screen and then tap **Send message**.

Respond to an Instant Message

When someone sends you an instant message, Windows 8 displays it on the Start screen, and you can then respond to the message. If the instant message is from one of your Windows account contacts or Facebook friends, Windows 8 displays a notification that shows you the name of the person and the message. On the Start screen, the Messaging tile is live, so it cycles through any unread instant messages that are waiting for you.

You can respond to an instant message using either the notification or the Start screen Messaging tile.

Respond to an Instant Message

Using a Notification

Ⓐ When an instant message arrives, Windows 8 displays a notification.

❶ Tap the notification.

Ⓑ The Messaging app opens and displays the conversation.

❷ Type your message.

❸ Tap **Enter**.

Messaging sends the response.

Using the Messaging Tile

C When you have new instant messages, the Messaging tile cycles through them.

D This number tells you the number of unread messages.

1 Tap the Messaging tile.

Windows 8 opens the Messaging app.

2 Tap the conversation.

3 Type your message.

4 Tap **Enter**.

Messaging sends the response.

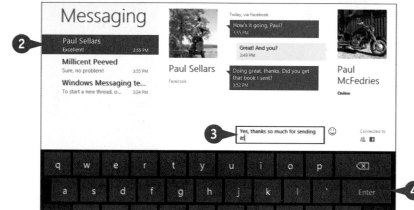

Can I prevent people from sending me instant messages?

Yes, you can change your instant messaging status so that other people cannot see you. To do this, follow these steps:

1 Open the Messaging app.

2 Swipe up from the bottom of the screen.

3 Tap **Status**.

4 Tap **Invisible**.

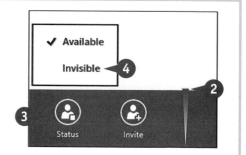

Messaging prevents people from sending you messages or even seeing that you are online.

CHAPTER 6

Getting Social with Your Tablet

You can use the People app to store contact information, connect to social networks, and keep track of friends. You can use the Calendar app to schedule meetings, appointments, and other events.

Create a Contact

You can easily store information about your friends, family, and colleagues, as well as send messages to them, by using the People app to create a contact for each person. Each contact can store a wide variety of information, such as a person's first and last names, company name, e-mail address, phone number, and street address.

If you already have contacts on a social network such as Facebook or LinkedIn, you do not need to enter those contacts by hand. Instead, you can connect your social network account to your Microsoft account, as described in the next few sections.

Create a Contact

1 On the Start screen, tap **People**.

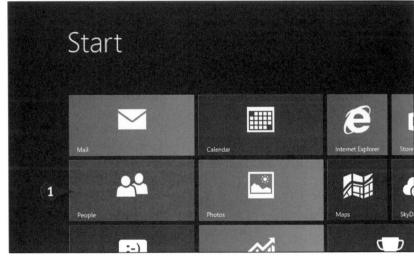

The People app loads.

2 Swipe up from the bottom edge of the screen.

3 Tap **New**.

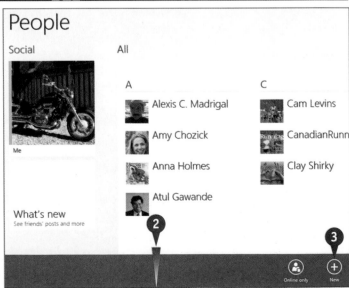

The New Contact screen appears.

④ Type the contact's first name.

⑤ Type the contact's last name.

⑥ Type the contact's company name.

⑦ Tap the **Email** label and then tap the type of e-mail address that you want to enter.

⑧ Type the contact's e-mail address.

⑨ Tap the **Phone** label and then tap the type of phone number that you want to enter.

⑩ Type the contact's phone number.

⑪ To add an address for the contact, tap the **Address** ⊕.

Ⓐ To add another field for the contact, tap ⊕, tap a label, and then type the data in the field that appears.

⑫ Tap **Save**.

The People app creates the new contact.

New contact

Account

Live

Name
First name
Chuck ← ④

Last name
Aster ← ⑤

Company
UCC Communications ← ⑥

⊕ Name

Email
Work ⌄ ⑦
caster@uccc.com ← ⑧

⊕ Email

Phone
Mobile ⌄

⊕ Phone

Address
⊕ Address

Other info
⊕ Other info

New contact

Account

Live

Name
First name
Chuck

Last name
Aster

Company
UCC Communications

⊕ Name

Email
Work ⌄
caster@uccc.com

⊕ Email

Phone ← ⑨
Mobile ⌄ ⑨
317-555-4321| ← ⑩ ✕

⊕ Phone
Ⓐ

Address
⑪ → ⊕ Address

Other info
⊕ Other info

⑫
⊟
Save

TIPS

Is there an easy way to send an e-mail to a contact?

Yes. Normally, you would open the Mail app, begin a new message as described in Chapter 5, "Sending E-mail and Messages," and then tap the **To** button to open the People app and choose a recipient. If you are already working in the People app, however, it is easier and faster to tap the person's tile to open the contact and then tap **Send email**.

Are there other types of information that I can record for a contact?

Yes, you can also add notes about the contact, the contact's job title, the contact's website address, and the name of the contact's significant other. To add one of these categories, tap the **Other info** ⊕, tap the category you want to add, and then type the information in the new field that appears.

Connect to Facebook

If you are using a Microsoft account with Windows 8, you can connect your Facebook account to your Microsoft account and see your Facebook friends in the People app. To do so, you must tell Facebook that you give permission to connect your Microsoft and Facebook accounts.

After you have connected your accounts, you can use the People app to view your friends' Facebook profiles, see the latest status updates and photos from your Facebook friends, and send messages to online Facebook friends.

Connect to Facebook

1 On the Start screen, tap **People**.

The People app loads.

2 Tap **Connected to**.

The Accounts pane appears.

3 Tap **Add an account**.

4 Tap **Facebook**.

The People app displays a description of the Facebook connection.

5 Tap **Connect**.

Facebook prompts you to log in to your account.

6 Type your Facebook e-mail address.

7 Type your Facebook password.

8 Select the **Keep me logged in** check box (☐ changes to ☑).

9 Tap **Log In**.

Windows 8 connects your Facebook account to your Microsoft account.

10 Tap **Done**.

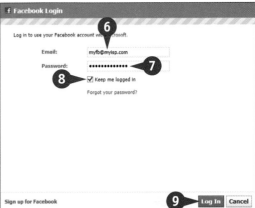

TIP

Can I interact with the Facebook messages that I receive in the People app?
Yes. See the section "View Your Contacts' Activities" later in this chapter to learn how to view Facebook posts. To "like" a Facebook post, locate it and then tap **Like**. To comment on a Facebook post, locate it, tap **Comment**, type your feedback, and then tap **Comment**.

Connect to Twitter

If you are using a Microsoft account with Windows 8, you can connect your Twitter account to your Microsoft account and see the people that you follow in the People app. To do so, you must tell Twitter that you give permission to connect your Microsoft and Twitter accounts.

After you have connected your accounts, you can use the People app to view the Twitter profiles of the people you follow, see their latest tweets, retweet posts, and send replies.

Connect to Twitter

1 On the Start screen, tap **People**.

The People app loads.

2 Tap **Connected to**.

The Accounts pane appears.

3 Tap **Add an account**.

4 Tap **Twitter**.

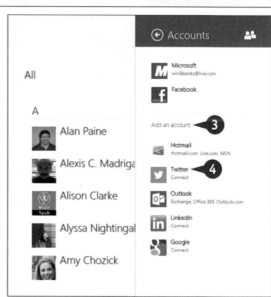

The People app displays a description of the Twitter connection.

5 Tap **Connect**.

Twitter prompts you to authorize the connection.

6 Type your Twitter username.

7 Type your Twitter password.

8 Select the **Remember me** check box (☐ changes to ☑).

9 Tap **Authorize app**.

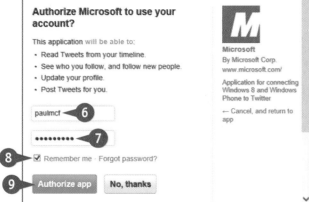

Windows 8 connects your Twitter account to your Microsoft account.

10 Tap **Done**.

TIP

Can I interact with the Twitter messages that I receive in the People app?
Yes. See the section "View Your Contacts' Activities" later in this chapter to learn how to view Twitter messages. To retweet a post, locate it and then tap **Retweet**. To set a tweet as a favorite, locate it and then tap **Favorite**. To send a message to the person who posted a tweet, locate the tweet, tap **Reply**, type your message, and then tap **Reply**.

Connect to LinkedIn

$\mathbf{I}$f you are using a Microsoft account with Windows 8, you can connect your LinkedIn account to your Microsoft account and see your LinkedIn connections in the People app. To do so, you must tell LinkedIn that you give permission to connect your Microsoft and LinkedIn accounts.

After you have connected your accounts, you can use the People app to view the LinkedIn profiles of the people to whom you are connected. You can also send an e-mail message to a connection and map a connection's address.

Connect to LinkedIn

1 On the Start screen, tap **People**.

The People app loads.

2 Tap **Connected to**.

The Accounts pane appears.

3 Tap **Add an account**.

4 Tap **LinkedIn**.

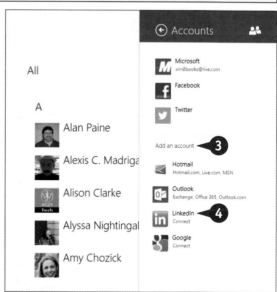

The People app displays a description of the LinkedIn connection.

5 Tap **Connect**.

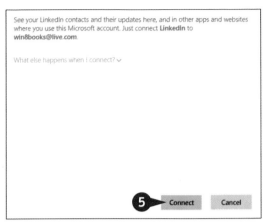

LinkedIn prompts you to authorize the connection.

6 Type your LinkedIn e-mail address.

7 Type your LinkedIn password.

8 Tap **Ok, I'll Allow It**.

Windows 8 connects your LinkedIn account to your Microsoft account.

9 Tap **Done**.

TIPS

Can I adjust the permissions set up between my Microsoft account and a social networking account?

Yes, each social network offers several different types of permission, and Windows 8 sets up default permissions at first. To change the default permissions, tap **Connect to**, tap the account that you want to adjust, and then tap **Manage this account online**. Use the check boxes to turn permissions on (☑) and off (☐) and then tap **Save**.

How do I disconnect a social network?

If you no longer use a social network in the People app, you should disconnect the network to reduce clutter in the app. Tap **Connect to**, tap the account that you want to adjust, tap **Remove this connection completely**, and then tap **Remove**.

Add Your Google Account

You can add your Google account to Windows 8 to access your Google contacts, e-mail, and calendar from your Windows 8 tablet. To do so, you must provide Windows 8 with your Google account login data.

After you have added your Google account, you can use the People app to view your Google contacts. You can use the Calendar app to view your Google events and appointments, and you can use the Mail app to view your Gmail messages.

Add Your Google Account

1 On the Start screen, tap **People**.

The People app loads.

2 Tap **Connected to**.

The Accounts pane appears.

3 Tap **Add an account**.

4 Tap **Google**.

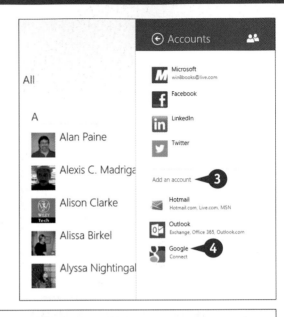

The People app prompts you for your Google login data.

5 Type your Google e-mail address.

6 Type your Google password.

7 Tap **Connect**.

Windows 8 connects your Google account to your Microsoft account.

TIP

Can I control what type of Google content appears in Windows 8?
Yes, you can configure the type of content to sync between Google and Windows 8 and how much of that content to sync:

1 In the People app, tap **Connected to**.

2 Tap **Google**.

3 Tap the **Download new content** ⌄ and set when Google items are synced.

4 Tap the **Download content from** ⌄ and set how much content is synced.

5 Tap **Email** (☑ changes to ☐) if you do not want to sync Gmail messages.

6 Tap **Contacts** (☑ changes to ☐) if you do not want to sync Google contacts.

7 Tap **Calendar** (☑ changes to ☐) if you do not want to sync Google events.

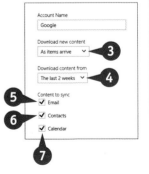

View a Contact

After you have added contacts and connected your other accounts to Windows 8, you can use the People app to view your contacts. The information that you see when you view a contact depends on how the contact was added to Windows 8. If you added the contact yourself, you see the information that you entered. If the contact was added by connecting another account to Windows 8, you see the data provided by that account.

After you have a contact displayed, you can edit the contact's data to update existing information or add new information.

View a Contact

View a Contact

1 On the Start screen, tap **People**.

The People app loads.

2 Locate and then tap the contact.

Ⓐ The People app displays the contact's data.

③ When you are done with the contact, tap ⊙ to return to the People tab.

Edit a Contact

① Swipe up from the bottom edge of the screen.

② Tap **Edit**.

③ Make your changes to the contact's data.

④ Tap **Save**.

The People app saves the updated data.

TIP

Is there an easier way to view a contact that I use frequently?

Yes, Windows 8 gives you a couple of methods for quickly accessing frequently used contacts. Follow steps **1** to **3** in this section to open the contact and then swipe up from the bottom of the screen to reveal the application bar. Tap **Pin to Start**, edit the contact name as necessary, and then tap **Pin to Start**. This adds a tile for the contact to the Start screen.

Alternatively, follow steps **1** to **3** in this section to open the contact, swipe up from the bottom to open the application bar, and then tap **Favorite**. This adds the contact to the beginning of the People tab.

View Your Contacts' Activities

After you have connected your Microsoft account to one or more social network accounts, you can use the People app to view contact activities such as Facebook posts and photos and Twitter updates.

One of Microsoft's goals when designing the Windows 8 Start screen was to give you a single place that shows you what is happening in your life. The People app can show you the latest messages from your social networks. You can view messages for all contacts or just a single contact.

View Your Contacts' Activities

View All Contacts' Activities

1 Tap **What's new**.

Note: If you do not see the What's New section, swipe up from the bottom of the screen and tap **Home**.

A Your latest messages appear.

View One Contact's Activities

1 Swipe up from the bottom of the screen.

2 Tap **Home**.

3 Tap the contact.

4 Swipe left to the **What's new** section.

B The contact's latest activity appears here.

C Tap **View all** to see more activities.

TIPS

Can I see a friend's Facebook photos in the People app?

Yes, the People app shows each friend's Facebook photo albums, including his or her profile pictures and wall photos. To view a friend's Facebook photos, follow steps **1** to **3** in the "View One Contact's Activities" subsection to open the contact for your Facebook friend. Swipe left to **Photos** section and then tap the album that you want to view.

Can I view a contact's Facebook or Twitter profile?

Yes, the People app offers links to the profiles of your Facebook friends and to the people that you follow on Twitter. In the What's New section, tap the person's name or Twitter handle to open his or her data screen. Otherwise, use the People section to tap the contact. Then tap **View profile** to switch to Internet Explorer and display the contact's profile.

View Your Social Networking Activity

A fter you have connected your Microsoft account to one or more social network accounts, you can use the People app to view your recent social networking activity.

Your social networking activity includes your Facebook status updates, posts, and photos, as well as your Twitter updates and retweets. Your activity also includes any notifications that a social networking service sends you. These notifications include comments on your Facebook posts, Twitter mentions, and service messages.

View Your Social Networking Activity

1 Tap the **People** tile.

The People app appears.

Ⓐ This number tells you how many of your recent social network notifications you have yet to view.

2 Tap **Me**.

B Your latest social network post appears here.

C Tap **View all** to see all your recent posts.

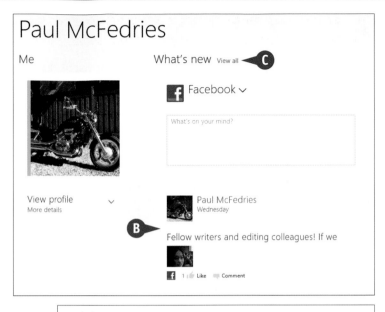

Paul McFedries

Me   What's new View all **C**

f Facebook ∨

What's on your mind?

View profile
More details   ∨

Paul McFedries
Wednesday

B

Fellow writers and editing colleagues! If we

f 1 👍 Like 💬 Comment

3 Swipe left.

D The Notifications section shows the recent notifications sent by your social networks.

E The Photos section shows your social network photo albums.

← **Paul McFedries**

D Notifications 3 unread   **E** Photos 7 albums

Siobhan Farrell likes your post.
Thursday via Facebook

Cindy Riskin likes Paul McFedries.
Thursday via Facebook

RT @paulmcf: Fellow writers and editing colleagues!
If we work hard, we can get to #1 on this list of the
Wednesday via Twitter

Jane Farrow posted in Tim & Taylor's Quarter Century
KURFUFFLE: "Congrats on the kerfuffle. I b   in the
Tuesday via Facebook   **3**

Norman Clifton likes Paul McFedries.
Monday via Facebook

Measuring the impact of #tweets by @paulmcf
http://t.co/M6YhYk9I #altmetrics #twimpact
Monday via Twitter

Profile Pictures

Gypsy, the Best Dog Ever!

TIP

Can I use a Facebook photo as my lock screen background?

Yes. On the Start screen, tap **Photos** to open the Photos app. Tap **Facebook** to display your Facebook albums, tap the album that contains the photo that you want to use, and then tap the photo to open it. Swipe up from the bottom of the screen to display the application bar, tap **Set as**, and then tap **Lock screen**.

Note that you can also use a Facebook photo as the Photos app background by opening the photo, tapping **Set as**, and then tapping **App background** or as the Photos tile background by opening the photo, tapping **Set as**, and then tapping **App tile**.

Post a Link to a Social Network

If you come across an interesting, useful, or entertaining web page, you can share that page by posting the link to a social network.

Windows 8 does not offer any way to post a text-only Facebook status update or tweet. However, you can use the Share feature to post links to interesting web pages. You can post a link and a short message describing the web page to your Facebook feed or to your Twitter followers.

Post a Link to a Social Network

1. Use Internet Explorer to open the web page that you want to share.

2. Swipe left from the right edge of the screen.

The Charms menu appears.

3. Tap **Share**.

The Share pane appears.

④ Tap **People**.

Windows 8 displays a new social network message.

Ⓐ A link to the web page appears here.

⑤ Tap ☑ and select **Facebook** or **Twitter**.

⑥ Type a message introducing or describing the link.

⑦ Tap the Send button (🖼).

Windows 8 posts the link to the social network.

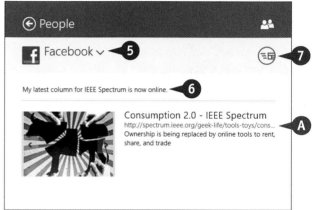

TIP

Can I share other types of content in addition to links to my social networks?
Yes, several other apps support sharing data to Facebook and Twitter. For example, you can use the Music app to open an album — either one of your own or one in the store — and then post information about the artist to your friends or followers. You can also use the Video app to share information about a movie or TV show, the Store app to share a link to an app in the Windows Store, and the Maps app to share a map or directions to a location.

View Your Calendar

Windows 8 comes with a Calendar app to enable you to manage your schedule. To create an event such as an appointment, meeting, or an all-day event such as a conference or trip, you first select the date when the event occurs.

You can change the calendar view. For example, you can show just a single day's worth of events if you want to concentrate on that day's activities. Similarly, you can view a week's or a month's worth of events if you want to get a larger sense of what your overall schedule looks like.

View Your Calendar

View Events by Month

1. On the Start screen, tap the **Calendar** tile.

2. Swipe up from the bottom of the screen.

3. Tap **Month**.

   Your calendar for the month appears.

4. Slide left and right to navigate the months.

View Events by Week

1. Swipe up from the bottom of the screen.

2. Tap **Week**.

   Your events for the week appear.

3. Slide left and right to navigate the weeks.

CHAPTER 6

View Events by Day

1 Swipe up from the bottom of the screen.

2 Tap **Day**.

The events for two days appear.

3 Slide left and right to navigate the days.

View Today's Events

1 Swipe up from the bottom of the screen.

2 Tap **Today**.

Calendar navigates the current view to include today's date.

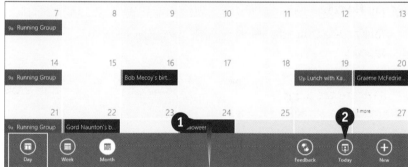

 TIP

Are there any shortcuts that I can use to navigate the calendar?

Yes, if you are using a tablet PC with a keyboard, the Calendar app offers several keyboard shortcuts that you can use to change the view:

Press	To
Ctrl + 1	Switch to Day view.
Ctrl + 2	Switch to Week view.
Ctrl + 3	Switch to Month view.
Ctrl + T	View today's events.
→	Navigate to the next screen in the current view.
←	Navigate to the previous screen in the current view.

Add an Event to Your Calendar

You can help organize your life by using the Calendar app to record your upcoming events — such as appointments, meetings, phone calls, and dates — on the date and time that they are scheduled to occur.

If the event has a set time and duration — for example, a meeting or a lunch date — you add the event directly to the calendar as a regular appointment. If the event has no set time — for example, a birthday, anniversary, or multiple-day event such as a sales meeting or vacation — you can create an all-day event.

Add an Event to Your Calendar

1 In the Calendar app, navigate to the date when the event occurs.

2 Tap the time when the event starts.

Note: If you are currently in Month view, tap the day the event occurs.

Note: You can also start a new event by swiping up from the bottom edge of the screen and then tapping **New**.

Calendar displays the New Event screen.

3 Type a name for the event.

4 Type the event location.

5 If the start time is incorrect, use the **Start** controls to select the correct time.

6 Tap the **How long** ⌄.

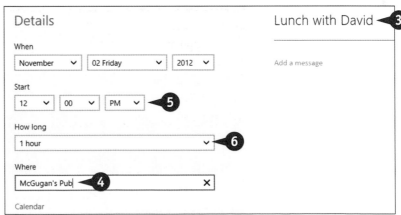

7 Tap the duration of the event.

A If the event is an anniversary or other event that lasts all day, tap **All day**.

B To choose a specific end time, tap **Custom** (see the Tip below).

8 Use the large text area to type notes related to the event.

9 Tap the Save This Event button (⊞).

C Calendar adds the event to your schedule.

D To make changes to the event, tap it.

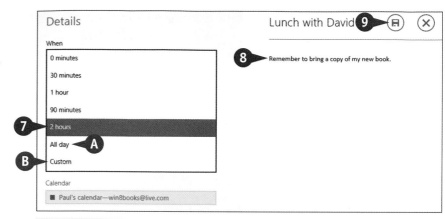

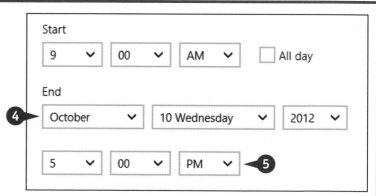

TIP

How do I create a custom event duration?

With a custom event duration, you specify not only the date and time the event starts, but also the date and time the event ends. Here are the steps to follow:

1 Follow steps **1** to **5** to set up a new event or tap an existing event.

2 Tap the **How long** ⌄.

3 Tap **Custom**.

Calendar adds controls for the end of the event.

4 Use these controls to set the end date.

5 Use these controls to set the end time.

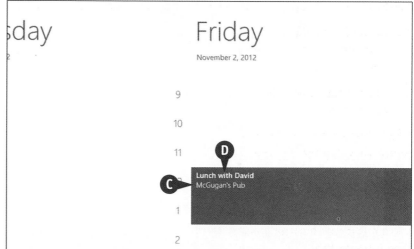

Create a Recurring Event

If you have an activity or event that recurs at a regular interval, you can create an event and configure it to automatically repeat in the Calendar app. This saves you from having to repeatedly add the future events yourself because Calendar adds them for you automatically.

You can repeat an event daily, weekly, monthly, or yearly. If your activity recurs every day only during the work week, such as a staff meeting, you can also set up the event to repeat every weekday.

Create a Recurring Event

1 Follow the steps in the preceding section, "Add an Event to Your Calendar," to create an event.

2 Tap **Show more**.

3 Tap the **How often** ⊡.

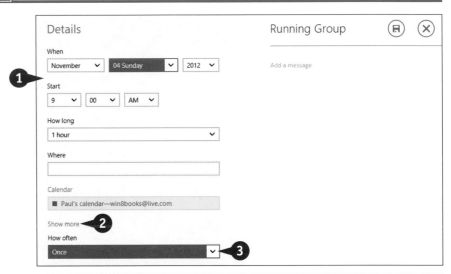

4 Tap the repeat interval that you want to use.

5 Tap ⊡.

Calendar adds the future events using the interval that you specified.

Note: To edit a recurring event, tap it and then tap either **Change one** to edit just that occurrence or **Change all** to edit every occurrence.

Add an Event Reminder

We are all living hectic, busy lives, and with our schedules more crammed than ever, it is easy to forget about an upcoming appointment or anniversary. You can help make sure that you never miss a meeting, appointment, or other event by setting up the Calendar app to remind you before the event occurs. A *reminder* is a notification message that Windows 8 displays at a specified time before the event occurs.

Add an Event Reminder

1 Follow the steps in the section "Add an Event to Your Calendar," earlier in this chapter, to create an event.

2 Tap **Show more**.

3 Tap the **Reminder** ⊡.

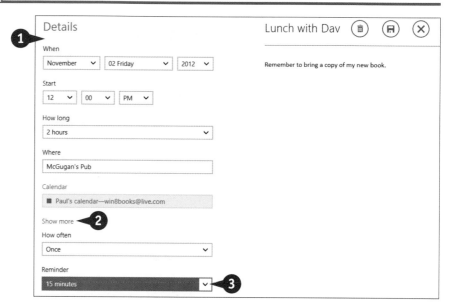

4 Tap the length of time before the event that you want the reminder to appear.

5 Tap ⊡.

Calendar saves the event and later reminds you of it beforehand, according to the time that you selected.

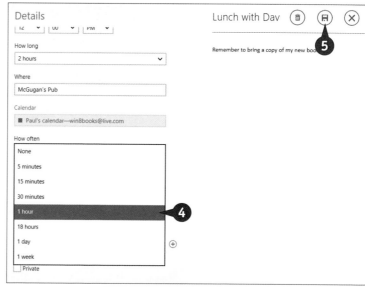

Send or Respond to an Event Invitation

The Calendar app has a feature that enables you to include people from your Contacts list in your event by sending them invitations to attend. If you receive an event invitation yourself, you can respond to it to let the person organizing the event know whether you will be attending.

The advantage of this approach is that when other people respond to the invitation, Calendar automatically updates the event. When you receive an event invitation, the e-mail message contains buttons that enable you to respond quickly.

Send or Respond to an Event Invitation

Send an Event Invitation

1 Follow the steps in the section "Add an Event to Your Calendar," earlier in this chapter, to create an event.

2 Tap **Show more**.

3 In the **Who** list, type the e-mail addresses of the people that you want to invite.

Note: To invite multiple people, separate the e-mail addresses with commas.

4 Tap 🗹.

The invitation is sent.

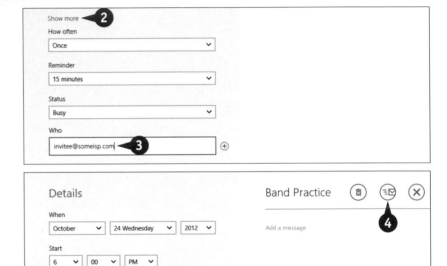

Handle an Event Invitation

1 On the Start screen, tap **Internet Explorer**.

2 Type **mail.live.com** and tap ◉.

Your Inbox appears.

3 Tap the invitation message.

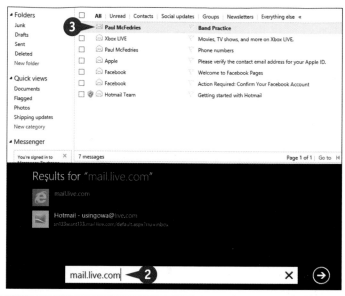

4 Tap the button that represents your reply to the invitation:

Ⓐ Tap **Accept** if you can attend the event.

Ⓑ Tap **Decline** if you cannot attend the event.

Ⓒ Tap **Tentative** if you are currently not sure whether you can attend.

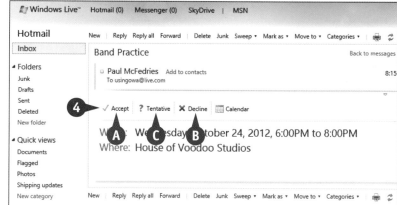

TIPS

After I receive an event invitation, is there a quick way to add the event to my calendar?
Yes. If you tap **Accept** in the invitation message, Hotmail automatically adds the event to your account calendar. The next time you open Windows 8's Calendar app, you will see the event at the date and time it is scheduled to occur.

If I am not sure whether to accept or decline an invitation, is there a quick way to check my calendar?
Yes. The invitation message includes a link to your calendar that automatically displays the date on which the event occurs. Tap the message and then tap **Calendar**. Internet Explorer switches to the Live Calendar page and displays the event date so that you can check your schedule.

CHAPTER 7

Working with Multimedia

If you are into photos, movies, TV shows, music, or games, you will appreciate the Windows 8 apps that help you view, organize, edit, and generally get the most out of your multimedia. This chapter gives you the details on all of Windows 8's media apps.

Import Images from a Digital Camera

You can import photos from a digital camera and save them on your tablet. If your camera stores the photos on a memory card, you can also use a memory card reader attached to your tablet to upload the digital photos from the removable drive that Windows 8 sets up when you insert the card. To perform the import directly from your digital camera, you need a cable to connect your camera to your tablet. Most digital cameras come with a USB cable.

After you have the digital photos on your system, you can view or print the images.

Import Images from a Digital Camera

1 Plug in your camera or memory storage card reader.

A notification appears.

2 Tap the notification.

Windows 8 displays a list of actions that you can perform.

3 Tap **Import photos and videos**.

The Photos app loads and selects all the photos that are on your camera.

4 Tap any photo that you do not want to import.

5 Type a name for the folder where the photos will be imported.

6 Tap **Import**.

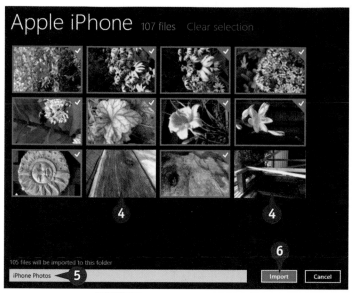

Windows 8 begins importing the photos.

7 When the import is complete, tap **Open album**.

The Photos app displays your imported photos.

TIP

What do I do if I want to import only a few of the photos on my camera?

If the photos on your camera represent several different events or themes, you might not want to import everything into a single folder. Instead, a better method is to import each collection of related photos into its own folder.

If you have many photos but only want to import a few of them, it can be time-consuming to deselect every photo that you do not want to import. Instead, tap **Clear selection** to remove the selection from all the photos and then tap just the ones that you want to import.

Follow steps **5** to **7** in this section to complete the import and then swipe up from the bottom of the Photos screen. Tap **Import** and then tap your camera to return to the import screen. Note that Photos automatically deselects any photos that you have already imported.

Navigate the Pictures Library

Before you can work with your images, you need to view them on your tablet. You do that by using the Photos app to open the Windows 8 Pictures library, which is a special folder designed specifically for storing images.

To get more out of the Pictures library, you need to know the basic techniques for opening any albums that you have stored in it. If you want to view your Facebook or Flickr albums in Windows 8, see the section "View Your Facebook Photos" or "View Your Flickr Photos" later in this chapter.

Navigate the Pictures Library

1 On the Start Screen, tap **Photos**.

The Photos app loads.

2 Tap **Pictures library**.

The Pictures library appears.

Ⓐ Items with names are albums that contain multiple images.

Ⓑ Items without names are individual images.

③ Tap an album.

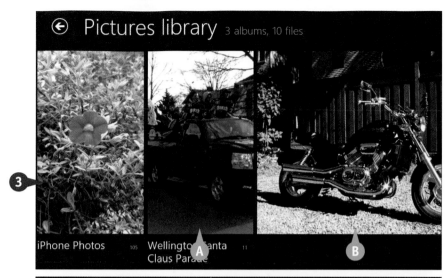

The album appears.

Ⓒ You can tap 🔄 to return to the previous section of the Photos app.

TIP

Can I change the image that appears as the background of the main Photos screen?
Yes, to do so, follow these steps:

① Follow the steps in this section to locate the image that you want to use.

② Tap the image to open it.

③ Swipe up from the bottom edge of the screen.

The Photos application bar appears.

④ Tap **Set as**.

⑤ Tap **App background**.

The Photos app now uses your picture as its background image.

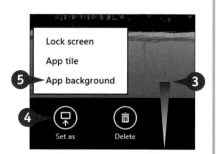

View Your Images

If you want to look at several images, the Photos app offers a couple tools that you can use to navigate backward and forward through the images in the Pictures library.

First, you can use the Photos app to open an album within your Pictures library, and you can then swipe through the images in that album. Second, you can open an album within your Pictures library and then open an individual image for viewing. You can then navigate through the other images in that album.

View Your Images

Swipe through an Album

1 Open the album that contains the images you want to view.

Note: See the preceding section, "Navigate the Pictures Library," for details.

A The Photos app displays the images in the album.

2 Swipe left.

The Photos app displays the next screenful of images from the album.

3 Repeat step **2** to continue viewing the album images.

B You can return to the previous screenful by swiping right.

View Individual Images

1 Open the album that contains the images you want to view.

Note: See the preceding section, "Navigate the Pictures Library," for details.

2 Tap the first image that you want to view.

The Photos app displays the image.

3 Swipe left to see the next image.

C You can return to the previous image by swiping right.

TIPS

Can I zoom in and out of a photo?
Yes, you should be able to do this on most tablets by using gestures. To zoom in, use the spread gesture — place two fingers close together on the screen and then spread them apart. To zoom back out, use the pinch gesture — place two fingers relatively far apart on the screen and then bring them together.

Can I rotate a photo?
Yes, you should be able to do this on most tablets by using the rotate gesture. Place two fingers relatively far apart on the screen and then turn them together in a circular motion. The image rotates in the same direction.

View Your Facebook Photos

If you are running Windows 8 with a Microsoft account and you have connected that account to your Facebook profile (see Chapter 6, "Getting Social with Your Tablet," for details), you can use the Photos app to view your Facebook photos.

After you open a Facebook photo album, you can swipe through the images in it. Alternatively, you could open just an individual image for viewing. You can then navigate through the other images in the same album.

View Your Facebook Photos

1 In the Photos app, tap **Facebook**.

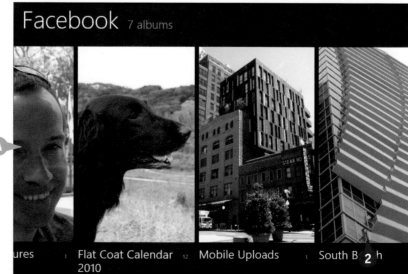

A Your Facebook photo albums appear.

2 Tap the album that contains the images you want to view.

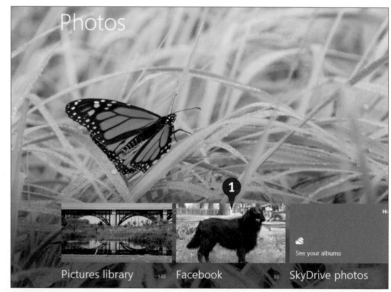

The Photos app displays the images in the album.

3 Swipe left and right to scroll through the album.

4 To view a specific image, tap it.

The image is displayed.

5 Swipe left to see the next image.

B You can return to the previous image by swiping right.

Can I use the Photos app to perform Facebook-specific tasks such as tagging people in photos?

No, the Photos app does not offer Facebook-specific photo features such as tagging and adding a location. To edit your photos using these features, you must use the Facebook website. However, the Photos app does give you an easy way to open a photo on Facebook:

1 Follow the steps in this section to open a Facebook photo.

2 Swipe up from the bottom of the screen.

3 Tap **View on Facebook**.

Windows 8 switches to Internet Explorer and displays the photo on the Facebook site. If you are not currently logged in to Facebook, you will need to log in before you can see the photo.

View Your Flickr Photos

If you are running Windows 8 with a Microsoft account, you can connect it to your Flickr account. After doing so, you can use the Photos app to open a Flickr photo album and then swipe through the images in that album. Alternatively, you can open just an individual image for viewing. You can then navigate through the other images in the same album.

View Your Flickr Photos

Connect to Your Flickr Account

1 In the Photos app, tap **Flickr photos**.

Windows 8 prompts you to connect to Flickr.

2 Tap **Connect**.

Windows 8 asks for your Yahoo! Sign-in data.

3 Type your Yahoo! ID.

4 Type your Yahoo! password.

5 Tap **Keep me signed in** (☐ changes to ☑).

6 Tap **Sign In**.

Yahoo! asks you to give permission for your Microsoft account to access your Flickr account.

7 Tap **Ok, I'll Authorize It.**

Yahoo! authorizes your Microsoft account.

8 Tap **Done.**

You can now view your Flickr photos within the Photos app.

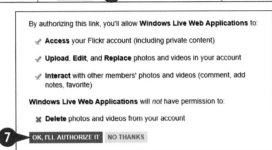

View Your Flickr Photos

1 In the Photos app, tap **Flickr photos**.

2 Follow the steps in the section "View Your Images" to navigate your Flickr albums and photos.

TIP

Can I use the Photos app to organize my Flickr photos into sets, add tags, and perform other tasks that I normally do on Flickr?

No, you cannot use the Photos app to perform Flickr-specific tasks. To organize and edit your photos using these features, you must use the Flickr website. Follow these steps to open a photo on Flickr directly from the Photos app:

1 Follow the steps in this section to open a Flickr photo.

2 Swipe up from the bottom of the screen.

3 Tap **View on Flickr.**

Windows 8 switches to Internet Explorer and displays the photo on the Flickr site. If you are not currently signed in to Yahoo!, you will need to sign in before you can see the photo.

Start a Slide Show

Instead of viewing your photos one at a time, you can easily view multiple photos by running them in a slide show. You can run the slide show from within the Photos app. The slide show displays each photo for a few seconds and then automatically moves on to the next photo.

Alternatively, you can view a slide show of images using the Photos tile on the Start screen. This slide show uses random images from your Pictures library and other connected photo libraries, such as Facebook and Flickr.

Start a Slide Show

In the Photos App

1 In the Photos app, open the library that you want to use.

2 Tap the album that contains the photos you want to display in your slide show.

The album appears.

3 Swipe up from the bottom of the screen.

The Photos application bar appears.

4 Tap **Slide show**.

The Photos app begins the slide show.

On the Photos Tile

1 In the Photos app, swipe left from the right edge of the screen.

The Charms menu appears.

2 Tap **Settings**.

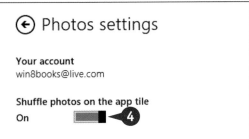

The Settings pane appears.

3 Tap **Settings**.

The Photos Settings pane appears.

4 Tap **Shuffle photos on the app tile** to **On**.

The next time that you display the Start screen, the Photos tile displays a slide show of random images from your libraries.

Note: If you do not see the images on the Photos tile, make sure that the Photos tile is live. Swipe down on the Photos tile and then tap **Turn live tile on**.

TIP

Can I change the speed at which the slide show images are displayed?
No, not with the Photos app. However, you can adjust the speed if you start the slide show from File Explorer on the desktop. Tap the **Desktop** tile, tap the File Explorer button (⬚), double-tap the **Pictures** library, and then double-tap the folder that you want to view. In the ribbon, tap the **Manage** tab and then tap **Slide show** to start the show. To control the speed, tap and hold the screen, release to display the shortcut menu, and then tap the speed that you want: **Slow**, **Medium**, or **Fast**.

Delete an Image

The images that you create may not always turn out perfectly. A photo may be blurry, or an edited image may not turn out the way that you wanted it to. When you are viewing an album or watching a slide show, having a bad image turn up can make the experience less pleasant. You can prevent that from happening by deleting an image you no longer want to work with or view. You can delete a single image or multiple images with a single command.

Delete an Image

Delete a Single Image

1 Open the image that you want to delete.

2 Swipe up from the bottom of the screen.

The Photos application bar appears.

3 Tap **Delete**.

The Photos app asks you to confirm the deletion.

4 Tap **Delete**.

The image is deleted.

Delete Multiple Images

1 Open the album that contains the images you want to delete.

2 Swipe down on each image that you want to delete.

A A check mark is added to indicate that the photo is selected.

B The Photos app updates the number of images selected.

Note: If you select an image by accident, swipe down on it again to deselect.

C To start over, tap **Clear selection**.

3 Tap **Delete**.

The Photos app asks you to confirm the deletion.

4 Tap **Delete**.

The image is deleted.

TIPS

I want to delete all but a few of the photos in an album. Is there an easy way to do that?
Yes, particularly if you are working with an album that contains a large number of images. Display the application bar by swiping up from the bottom of the screen. Tap **Select all** to select every image in the album and then swipe down on each image that you want to keep. Tap **Delete** and then tap **Delete** again when the Photos app asks you to confirm the deletion.

What can I do if I delete an image accidentally?
Windows 8 sends deleted images to the Recycle Bin, so in most cases, you can restore the image from that folder. On the Start screen, tap **Desktop** to open the Desktop app and then double-tap the **Recycle Bin** icon. In the Recycle Bin window, tap the image to select it, tap the **Manage** tab, and then tap **Restore the selected items**.

Take a Picture

If your tablet comes with a built-in camera or if you have an external camera attached to your tablet, you can use the camera to take a picture of yourself, someone else, your surroundings — anything you want — using the Camera app. The Camera app also gives you the option of recording a video.

The Camera app stores each photo or video in a new album called *Camera Roll,* which appears in your Pictures library.

Take a Picture

1 On the Start screen, tap **Camera**.

The first time that you start the Camera app, it asks for permission to use your tablet's camera and microphone.

2 Tap **Allow**.

The Camera app loads.

Ⓐ A live feed from the camera appears.

Ⓑ If you want to record a video, tap **Video Mode** to select it.

Ⓒ If you want the camera app to delay three seconds before taking the photo or starting the video recording, tap **Timer** to select it.

❸ When you are ready to take the photo or begin the recording, tap the screen.

The Camera app takes the photo or starts the recording.

❹ If you are recording a video, tap the screen when you are finished.

The Camera app saves your photo or video.

TIPS

I accidentally tapped Block when I first started the Camera app. How can I change this?
Open the Camera app, swipe left from the right edge of the screen to display the Charms menu, tap **Settings**, and then tap **Permissions** to open the Permissions pane. Under **Privacy**, tap the **Webcam and microphone** switch to **On**. Tap the Camera app and then tap **Change camera**.

My video recordings are shaky. Can I fix this?
Yes, in many cases. However, this depends on whether your tablet supports a feature called *video stabilization*, which can remove most of the artifacts caused by a shaking camera. To activate this feature, tap **Camera options** and then tap the **Video Stabilization** switch to **On**.

Navigate the Videos Library

Before you can work with your videos, you need to locate them on your tablet. You do that by using the Video app to open the Windows 8 Videos library, which is a special folder designed specifically for storing digital videos, movies, and recorded TV shows.

To get more out of the Videos library, you need to know the basic techniques for opening any videos that you have stored in it. If you are looking for commercial movies or TV shows, see the sections "Buy or Rent a Movie" and "Buy a TV Episode," later in this chapter.

Navigate the Videos Library

1 On the Start Screen, tap
Video.

The Video app loads.

2 Swipe right until you see
the My Videos section.

A The Video app displays a
selection of the videos on
your tablet.

3 Tap **my videos**.

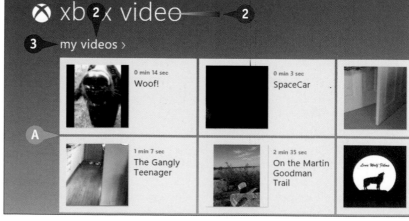

The Videos library appears.

④ Tap a video type.

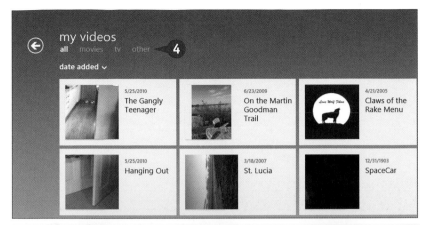

Ⓑ The digital videos of that type that you have on your tablet are displayed.

Ⓒ You can tap ⬅ to return to the previous section of the Video app.

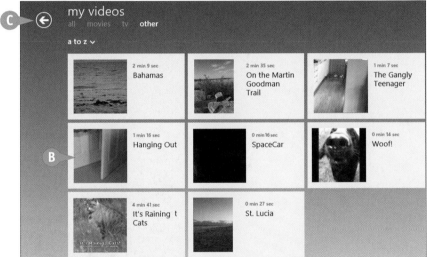

TIP

Why does the Video app not show the videos that I have recorded using the Camera app?
By default, the Camera app stores recorded videos in the Camera Roll folder, which is part of the Pictures library, whereas the Video app displays only digital video files from the Videos library. To have your Camera app videos appear in the Video app, you could use File Explorer (tap 📁 in the Desktop app) to move your recorded videos to the Videos library. Alternatively, in the Video app, tap **my videos**, swipe up from the bottom of the screen, tap **Open File**, tap **Files**, tap **Pictures**, tap **Camera Roll**, tap the video, and then tap **Open**.

Watch a Video

After you know how to use the Video app to navigate your Videos library, as shown in the preceding section, "Navigate the Videos Library," you can use the app to select and play a video that you have on your tablet. The Video app plays the video full screen on your tablet, so you get the best viewing experience. When you have the video playing, you can pause and restart the playback, and you can use a special tool called the *scrubber* to quickly fast forward or rewind the video to the spot that you want.

Watch a Video

Start a Video

1 Display your videos.

Note: See the preceding section for details.

2 Tap the tab that contains the video you want to play.

3 Tap the video.

The Video app begins playing the video.

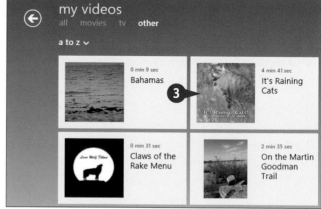

Control the Video Playback

1 Tap the screen.

The Video app displays the playback controls.

A Tap the Pause button to stop and restart the playback.

B Tap and drag the scrubber to rewind or fast-forward the video.

C Tap here to jump back in the video.

D Tap here to jump forward in the video.

TIP

Is there a way to get the video to automatically start over from the beginning?
Yes, the Video app offers a Repeat feature that automatically restarts the current video from the beginning as soon as the video ends. To activate this feature, follow these steps:

1 Start the video playback.

2 Swipe up from the bottom of the screen.

3 Tap **Repeat**.

Buy or Rent a Movie

You can use the Video app to purchase a movie to own it or to rent a movie temporarily. Either way, the Video app downloads the movie to your tablet, and you can then watch the movie.

To purchase or rent a movie using the Video app, you must have a Microsoft account, and you must have enough Microsoft points in your account to cover the purchase or rental. See the Tip on the facing page to learn how to obtain Microsoft points.

Buy or Rent a Movie

1 In the Video app, tap **movies store**.

The Movies Store screen appears.

2 Tap a section.

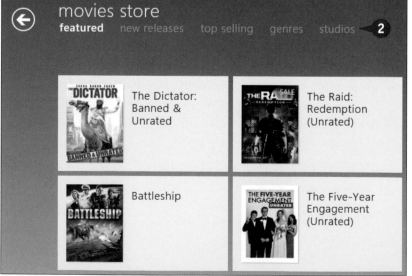

The Video app displays a selection of movies.

3 If the section contains subsections, tap here and then tap the subsection that you want to view.

4 Tap the movie that you want.

The Video app displays the movie's details.

5 Tap **Buy**.

Ⓐ If you prefer to rent the movie, tap **Rent** instead.

6 Select a download option and then click **Next**.

The Video app asks you to confirm the sale.

7 Tap **Confirm Purchase**.

The Video app finalizes the purchase and begins downloading the movie to your tablet.

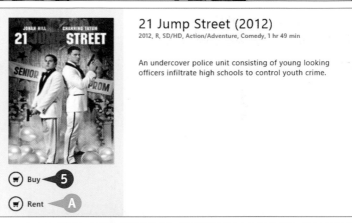

TIP

How do I get more Microsoft points?

You can obtain Microsoft points in several ways. For example, at a retail store that sells gift cards, you can purchase an Xbox LIVE points card and then redeem those points. You can also purchase Microsoft points online at http://xbox.live.com. Sign in to your account and then tap **Add Points**. To purchase points using the Video app, follow these steps:

1 In the Video app, swipe left from the right edge to open the Charms menu.

2 Tap **Settings**.

3 Tap **Account**.

4 Tap **Microsoft Points**.

5 Tap the number of points that you want to purchase (○ changes to ⦿).

6 Tap **Next**.

7 Select a payment method.

8 Tap **Confirm**.

Buy a TV Episode

You can use the Video app to purchase a TV episode to own it. After you make the purchase, the Video app downloads the episode to your tablet, and you can then watch the show. Note that you cannot rent a TV episode.

To purchase a TV episode using the Video app, you must have a Microsoft account, and you must have enough Microsoft points in your account to cover the purchase. See the Tip in the preceding section, "Buy or Rent a Movie," to learn how to obtain Microsoft points. See the Tip in this section to learn how to redeem an Xbox LIVE points card.

Buy a TV Episode

1 In the Video app, tap **television store**.

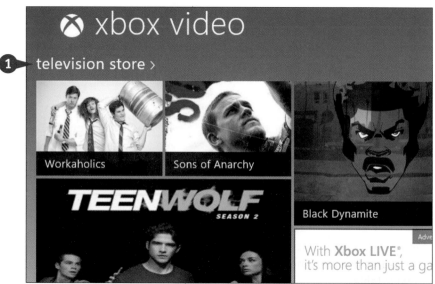

The Television Store screen appears.

2 Tap a section.

The Video app displays a selection of TV series.

Note: If the section contains subsections, tap the subsection that you want to view.

3 Tap the series that you want.

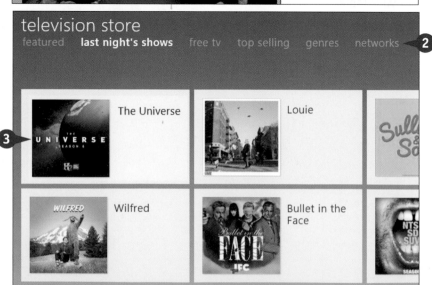

The Video app displays details about the series.

Note: If the Video app displays the series overview instead, tap **View Seasons** and then tap a season.

④ Tap the episode that you want to purchase.

⑤ Tap **Buy Episode**.

⑥ Select a download option and then click **Next**.

The Video app asks you to confirm the sale.

⑦ Tap **Confirm**.

The Video app finalizes the purchase and begins downloading the TV episode to your tablet.

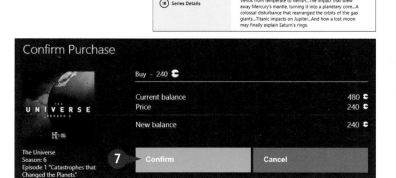

TIP

How do I redeem an Xbox LIVE points card?

If you have purchased an Xbox LIVE points card or received one as a gift, you can use the Video app to redeem it. In the Video app, follow these steps:

① Swipe left from the right edge to open the Charms menu.

② Tap **Settings**.

③ Tap **Account**.

④ Tap **Redeem Code**.

⑤ Type the 25-digit code found on the card.

⑥ Tap **Redeem Code**.

Navigate the Music Library

Before you can work with your songs and albums, you need to locate them on your tablet. You do that by using the Music app to open the Windows 8 Music library, which is a special folder designed specifically for storing digital music.

To get more out of the Music library, you need to know the basic techniques for opening any albums that you have stored in it. If you are looking for commercial albums or songs, see the section "Buy Music" later in this chapter.

Navigate the Music Library

1 On the Start Screen, tap **Music**.

The Music app loads.

2 Swipe right until you see the Music section.

A The Music app displays a selection of the albums on your tablet.

3 Tap **my music**.

The Music library appears.

④ Tap a music category.

Ⓑ The music in that
category appears.

Ⓒ You can tap Ⓖ to return
to the previous section
of the Music app.

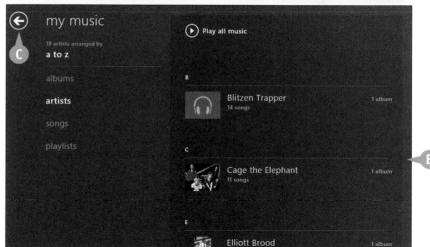

What can I do if a song that I want to play does not appear in the Music library?
By default, the Music app displays only digital music files from your user account's Music library. If your
song is outside of that library, the Music app will not see it. To fix this, you could use File Explorer (tap 🖼
in the Desktop app) to move your song from its current location to the Music library. Alternatively, in the
Music app, tap **my music**, swipe up from the bottom of the screen, tap **Open File**, tap **Files**, tap the
location of your song, tap the song, and then tap **Open**.

Play Music

If you want to listen to music while using your tablet, you can play tunes from your Music library. You can listen to all the songs on an album, all the songs from a particular artist, or individual songs. You can also play albums, artists, and songs in random order and play albums and artists repeatedly.

Windows 8 comes with three programs that you can use to play music: Windows Media Player and Windows Media Center are desktop programs covered in Chapter 8, "Performing Day-to-Day Tasks"; Music, a Windows 8 app, is the subject of this section.

Play Music

Start Music

1 Display your music.

Note: See the preceding section, "Navigate the Music Library," for details.

2 Tap the category that contains the music you want to play.

3 Tap the item that contains the music you want to play.

The Music app opens the item and displays a list of songs.

4 Tap **Play album**.

A You can also tap a song and then tap **Play**.

The selected music plays.

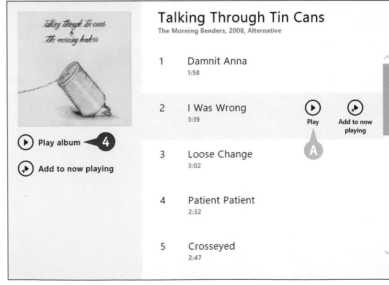

Control the Music Playback

1 Swipe up from the bottom of the screen.

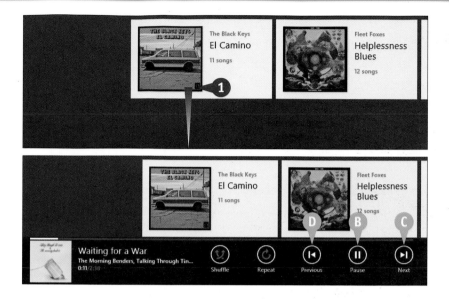

The Music app displays the playback controls.

B Tap **Pause** to stop and restart the playback.

C Tap **Next** to jump to the next song.

D Tap **Previous** to jump to the previous song.

Is there a way to get an album to automatically start over from the beginning?
Yes, the Music app offers a Repeat feature that automatically restarts the current album from the beginning as soon as the album ends. To activate this feature, follow these steps:

1 Start playing the album.

2 Swipe up from the bottom of the screen.

3 Tap **Repeat**.

Buy Music

You can use the Music app to purchase an album or a song to own it. After you make the purchase, the Music app downloads the album or song to your tablet, and you can then play the music.

To purchase an album or song using the Music app, you must have a Microsoft account, and you must have enough Microsoft points in your account to cover the purchase. See the Tip in the section "Buy or Rent a Movie" to learn how to obtain Microsoft points.

Buy Music

1 In the Music app, tap the category in which you want to make a purchase, such as **xbox music store** or **most popular**.

The Music app displays a selection of albums.

2 Tap a genre.

3 Tap a subgenre.

4 Tap an album.

The Video app displays the album details.

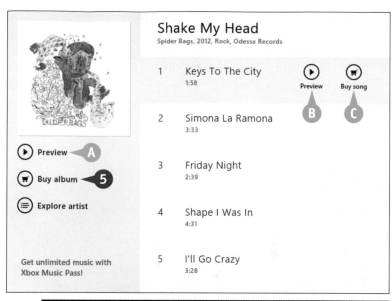

A Tap **Preview** to listen to samples of every song on the album.

B Tap a song and then tap **Preview** to hear a sample of that song.

5 Tap **Buy Album**.

C If you want to buy one song instead, tap the song and then tap **Buy Song**.

The Music app asks you to confirm the purchase.

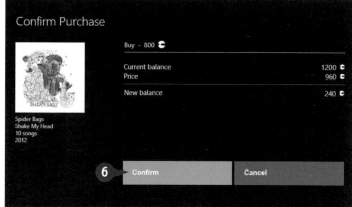

6 Tap **Confirm**.

The Music app finalizes the purchase and begins downloading the album or song to your tablet.

TIP

Can I search the Music app?

Yes, you can use Windows 8's Search feature to search for an artist, album, or song. In the Music app, swipe left from the right edge of the screen to open the Charms menu and then tap **Search**. In the Search pane, type all or part of the artist's name, album name, or song title. As you type, the Search pane displays the first few matches. If you see the artist, album, or song that you want, tap it to open it in the Music app.

Buy a Game

You can use the Games app to purchase a game to own it. After you make the purchase, the Games app downloads the game to your tablet, and you can then start playing the game.

To purchase a game using the Games app, you must have a Microsoft account, and you must have either a credit card or PayPal account assigned to your Microsoft account or enough Microsoft points in your account to cover the purchase. See the Tip to learn how to add PayPal or a credit card to your Microsoft account.

Buy a Game

1 On the Start screen, tap **Games**.

The Games app appears.

2 Tap **windows game store**.

The Windows Game Store screen appears.

3 Tap a section.

Games displays a selection of games.

A If the section contains subsections, tap the subsection that you want to view.

4 Tap the game that you want.

Games displays the game details.

5 Tap **Buy Game**.

Games asks you to confirm the purchase.

B If the game is relatively expensive, Games suggests using a credit card or PayPal account associated with your Microsoft account.

C Tap **Use Microsoft Points** if you would rather purchase the game using points.

6 Tap **Confirm**.

Games finalizes the purchase and downloads the game.

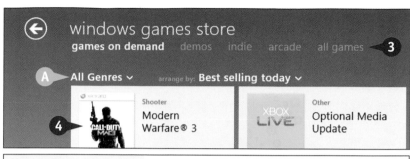

TIP

How do I add PayPal or a credit card to my Microsoft account?

Although you can use Microsoft points to purchase games, many are too expensive for that option. Instead, you can add PayPal or a credit card to your Microsoft account. For PayPal, sign in to your account at www.xbox.com, tap **My Account**, and then tap **Manage Payment Options**. For a credit card, follow these steps in the Games app:

1 Swipe left from the right edge to open the Charms menu.

2 Tap **Settings**.

3 Tap **Account**.

4 Tap **Manage Payment Options**.

5 Tap **Add a New Credit Card**.

The Add Credit Card pane appears.

6 Fill in your credit card type, number, expiration date, and verification code.

7 Fill in your personal data.

8 Tap **Save**.

Connect Your Tablet to Your Xbox

If you have an Xbox console connected to a TV, you might prefer to play your Windows 8 media on the larger screen. To do that, you can connect your tablet to your Xbox console and then send media from your tablet to the console. You can play all kinds of Windows 8 media, including videos, movies, TV show episodes, music, and games.

To connect your tablet to your Xbox console, you must install the Xbox SmartGlass app from the Windows Store, as described in Chapter 2, "Working with Apps."

Connect Your Tablet to Your Xbox

Connect to Your Xbox Console

1 On the Start screen, tap **Xbox SmartGlass**.

The Xbox SmartGlass app appears.

2 Configure your Xbox console to work with Xbox SmartGlass, as described in the Tip.

3 Tap **Get started**.

4 Click **Next**.

Xbox SmartGlass connects to the console.

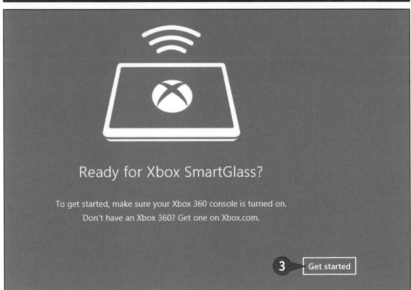

Play Media on your Xbox Console

1 In Xbox SmartGlass, tap the media that you want to play.

2 Tap **Play on Xbox 360**.

Xbox SmartGlass begins playing the media on your Xbox console.

The Babymakers
2012, R, SD/HD, Comedy, 1 hr 35 min

A man decides to rob a sperm bank with his friends when he has trouble conceiving a child with his wife.

(!) Play on Xbox 360 ◄ **2**

(≡) Explore movie

(▶) Play trailer

How do I configure my Xbox console for a connection to my tablet?

First turn on your Xbox console and make sure that the console is connected to the same network as your tablet. Then follow these steps to configure the Xbox console for connecting to your tablet:

1 Sign in to Xbox LIVE using the same Microsoft account that you use with Windows 8.

2 On the Xbox console, select **Settings**.

3 Select **System**.

4 Select **Console Settings**.

5 Select **Xbox Companion**.

6 Select **Available**.

Your Xbox console is now configured for connecting to your tablet.

CHAPTER 8

Performing Day-to-Day Tasks

You can use the Windows 8 apps to perform a number of useful day-to-day tasks, including searching for apps, settings, and files, getting directions to a location, looking up a weather forecast, planning a trip, tracking a stock, and getting the latest sports news. This chapter takes you through these tasks and more.

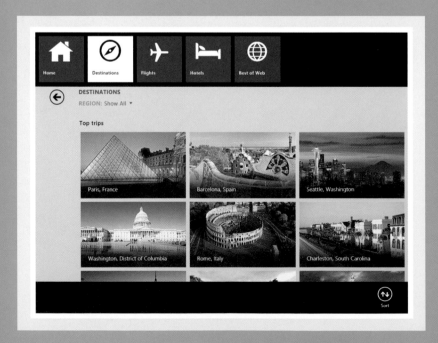

Search Your Tablet

After you have used your tablet for a while and have created many documents, you might have trouble locating a specific file. You can save a great deal of time by having Windows 8 search for your document. You can also use the Windows 8 Start screen to search for apps and system settings.

If you are working with the Desktop app, you can also perform file searches using the Search box in a folder window.

Search Your Tablet

Search for Apps

1 Swipe left from the right edge of the screen and then tap **Search**.

2 Tap **Apps**.

The Apps search screen appears.

3 Type your search text.

A Windows 8 displays each app with a name that includes your search text.

4 If you see the app that you want, tap it.

The app opens.

Search for Settings

1 Swipe left from the right edge of the screen and then tap **Search**.

2 Tap **Settings**.

The Settings search screen appears.

3 Type your search text.

B Windows 8 displays each setting that matches your search text.

4 If you see the setting that you want, tap it.

The setting opens.

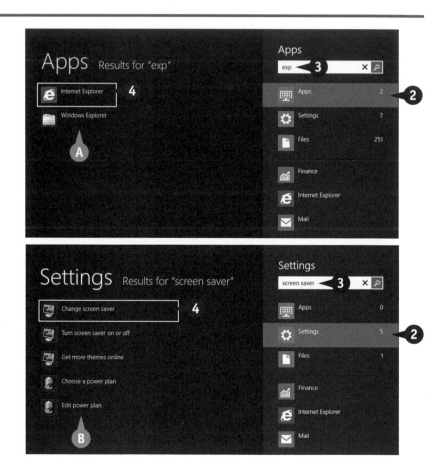

Search for Files

1 Swipe left from the right edge of the screen and then tap **Search**.

2 Tap **Files**.

3 Type your search text and then tap **Enter**.

C Windows 8 displays each file that matches your search text.

4 If you see the file that you want, tap it to open it.

Search from a Folder Window

1 Open the folder in which you want to search.

2 Type your search text.

D As you type, Windows 8 displays the folders and documents in the current folder with names, contents, or keywords that match your search text.

3 If you see the folder or document that you want, double-tap it.

The folder or document opens.

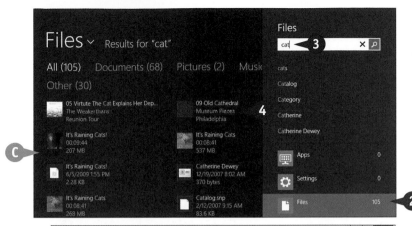
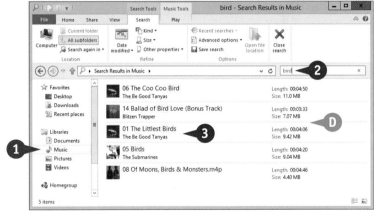

TIP

In Start screen searches, why does the search pane list various apps, such as Mail and Internet Explorer?

You can use those apps to tell Windows 8 that you want to run your search within the app itself. For example, if you want to search only your e-mail messages, type your search text and then tap **Mail**. Similarly, you can run a web search by typing your search text and then tapping **Internet Explorer**.

Display a Location on a Map

You can use the Maps app to display a location on a map. *Maps* is a Windows 8 app that displays digital maps that you can use to view just about any location by searching for an address or place name.

When you first start the Maps app, Windows 8 asks if it can turn on location services, which are background features that help determine your current location and offer this information to apps such as Maps. For the best results with Maps, you should allow Windows 8 to turn on location services.

Display a Location on a Map

1 On the Start screen, tap the **Maps** tile.

The first time that you start Maps, Windows 8 asks if it can turn on location services.

2 Tap **Allow**.

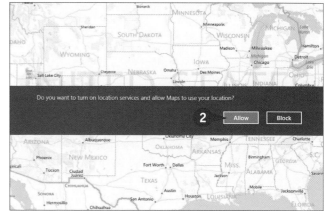

3 Swipe left from the right edge of the screen.

The Charms menu appears.

4 Tap **Search**.

The Search pane appears.

5 Type the address or the name of the location.

6 Tap the Search button (🔍).

Ⓐ Maps displays the location on the map.

Ⓑ If Maps displays multiple locations, tap the one that you want to view.

Note: To display your current location, swipe up from the bottom of the screen and then tap **My location**.

TIPS

How does the Maps app know my location?
The Maps app uses as many as three different bits of data to determine your location. First, it looks for known *Wi-Fi hotspots*, which are commercial establishments such as coffee shops that offer wireless Internet access. Second, if you are connected to the Internet, Maps uses the location information embedded in your unique Internet Protocol (IP) address. Third, if your tablet has a Global Positioning System (GPS) receiver, Maps uses this GPS data to pinpoint your location to within a few feet.

Can I turn off location services?
Yes. Swipe left from the right edge to open the Charms menu, tap **Settings**, and then tap **Change PC Settings**. In the PC Settings app, tap **Privacy** and then tap the **Let apps use my location** switch to **Off**.

Get Directions to a Location

esides displaying locations, Maps also understands the roads and highways found in most cities, states, and countries. This means that you can use the Maps app to get specific directions for traveling from one location to another. You specify a starting point and destination for a trip, and Maps then provides you with directions for getting from one point to the other. Maps highlights the trip route on a digital map and also gives you specific details for negotiating each leg of the trip.

Get Directions to a Location

1 Swipe up from the bottom of the screen.

The application bar appears.

2 Tap **Directions**.

Note: Maps assumes that you want to start at your current location. If that is true, skip step **3**.

3 Type the name or address of the location where your journey will begin.

4 Type the name or address of your destination.

5 Tap the Get Directions button (■).

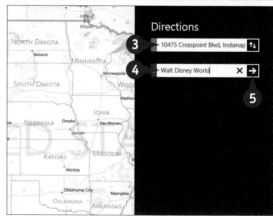

176

Ⓐ Maps displays an overview of your journey.

Ⓑ This area tells the distance and approximate traveling time by car.

Ⓒ This area displays the various legs of the journey.

❻ Tap the first leg of the trip.

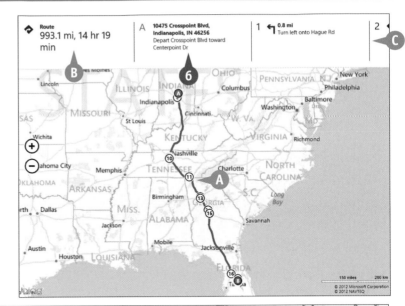

Ⓓ Maps zooms in to show you just that leg of the trip.

❼ As you complete each leg of the trip, tap the next leg for further instructions.

TIP

Can I get traffic information as I follow the directions provided by Maps?

Yes. Swipe up from the bottom edge of the screen to display the application bar. You can then tap **Show traffic** to see the current traffic conditions; green means traffic is moving normally, orange means traffic is slow, and red means traffic is heavy.

Check Your Weather Forecast

You can use the Weather app to view your city's current conditions and five-day forecast.

The Weather app takes advantage of Microsoft's Bing Weather service, which uses several online weather resources to obtain up-to-the minute conditions and forecasts. The Weather app includes a feature that uses Windows 8 location services to determine your location and display the forecast for your city. If you would prefer to see the forecast for some other city, see the following section, "Check Another City's Weather Forecast."

Check Your Weather Forecast

1. On the Start screen, tap **Weather**.

The Weather app appears.

2. Swipe down from the top of the screen.

The application bar appears.

3. Tap **Places**.

The Places screen appears.

4 Tap the Add button (⊕).

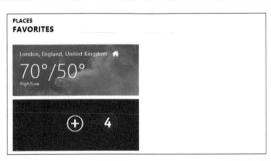

5 Tap the My Location button (◎).

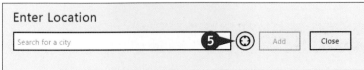

A Weather adds your city to the Places screen.

6 Tap your city.

Weather displays your current conditions and forecast.

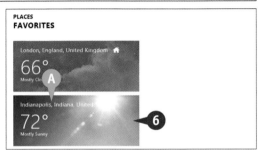

TIPS

Why, when I tap the My Location button, does the Weather app say, "Your location cannot be found"?

It means that you have turned off location services in Windows 8. To turn location services on, swipe left from the right edge to open the Charms menu, tap **Settings**, and then tap **Change PC Settings**. In the PC Settings app, tap **Privacy** and then tap the **Let apps use my location** switch to **On**.

I would like to see my city's forecast when I start the Weather app. How can I set this up?

If your city is the only one added to Weather, then you see your forecast as soon as you start the app. Otherwise, you need to make your location the default. To do this, follow steps **1** to **3** in this section to open the Places screen, swipe down on your location to select it, and then tap **Set as default**.

Check Another City's Weather Forecast

Y ou can use the Weather app to view another city's current conditions and five-day forecast.

The Bing Weather service use online resources to obtain up-to-the minute information on the current conditions and weather forecasts for hundreds of locations around the world. If you are going to be traveling to another city or if you are simply curious about the weather conditions elsewhere, you can use Maps to look up the weather forecast for most cities around the world.

Check Another City's Weather Forecast

1 In the Weather app, swipe down from the top of the screen.

The application bar appears.

2 Tap **Places**.

The Places screen appears.

3 Tap ⊕.

④ Type the name of the city whose weather you want to view.

Ⓐ As you type, Weather displays place names that match.

⑤ When you see the location that you want, tap it.

Ⓑ Weather adds the location to the Places screen.

⑥ Tap the location.

Weather displays the city's current conditions and forecast.

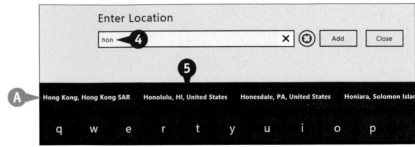

TIPS

Can I show the weather for more than one city on the Start screen?

Yes. By default, the Weather tile shows the current conditions for whatever city you have set up as the default location. To add a second Weather tile that shows the current conditions for another city, follow steps **1** and **2** in this section to open the Places screen, swipe down on the city that you want to add, tap **Pin**, and then tap **Pin to Start**.

How do I remove a city whose weather I no longer need to view?

To remove a location from the Places screen, first follow steps **1** and **2** in this section. Swipe down on the city that you want to remove and then tap **Remove**.

Plan a Trip

You can use the Travel app to plan your next vacation or business trip.

For the most part, we make our own travel arrangements nowadays, so it is useful to have tools such as this that can help plan each aspect of a trip. The Travel app offers features that enable you to research destinations and search for the best flights and hotels. The Travel app also offers travel articles, news, and tips, destination photos, lists of hotels and restaurants, travel guides, and more.

Plan a Trip

Start the Travel App

1. On the Start screen, tap **Travel**.

   The Travel app appears.

Note: On the Home page, you can slide left to see links to highlighted destinations, photos, and articles.

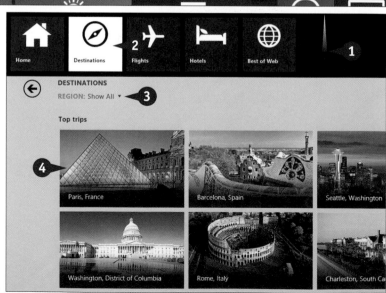

Research a Destination

1. Swipe down from the top edge of the screen.

2. Tap **Destinations**.

3. To narrow down the location, tap **Region** and then tap an area, such as **Europe** or **Caribbean**.

4. Tap the destination.

   The Travel app displays a screen that gives you an overview of the destination, as well as photos, lists of attractions, hotels, restaurants, and travel guides.

Search for Flights

1 Swipe down from the top edge of the screen.

2 Tap **Flights**.

3 Select your departure city.

4 Select your destination city.

5 Fill in your departure and return dates.

6 Select a cabin type.

7 Specify the number of passengers.

8 Tap **Search Flights**.

The Travel app displays a list of matching flights.

Search for Hotels

1 Swipe down from the top edge of the screen.

2 Tap **Hotels**.

3 Select your destination city.

4 Fill in your check-in and check-out dates.

5 Specify the number of rooms.

6 Specify the number of guests.

7 Tap **Search Hotels**.

The Travel app displays a list of matching hotels.

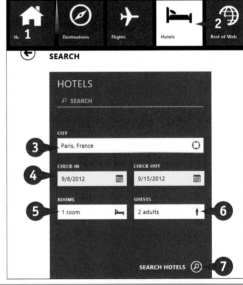

TIP

Is there a more direct way to locate a travel destination?

Yes, probably the easiest way is to search for it:

1 In the Travel app, swipe left from the right edge of the screen.

2 Tap **Search**.

3 Type the name of the location.

Ⓐ The Search pane displays a list of matching locations.

4 When you see the location that you want, tap it.

Get the Latest News

You can use the News app to read the latest news stories and to locate stories that are important to you.

The News app aggregates news stories from a wide variety of web sources, including the Associated Press, Reuters, *The New York Times*, and CNN. The News app's main page — called *Bing Daily* — displays stories in various categories, including Technology, Business, Politics, and Sports. If you are interested in other topics, you can customize the My News section to show stories related to those topics.

Get the Latest News

1 On the Start screen, tap **News**.

The News app appears.

2 In the Bing Daily page, swipe left and right to see the main stories of the day in each category.

3 Swipe down from the top of the screen.

The application bar appears.

4 Tap **My News**.

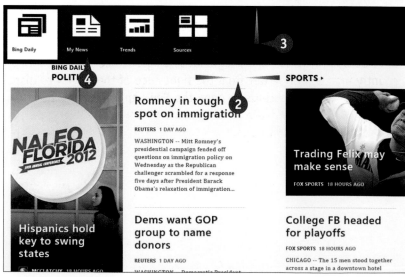

The My News page appears.

5 Tap the Add a Section button (◉).

Note: You can also swipe down from the top edge of the screen and tap **Add a section**.

The Add a Section screen appears.

6 Type the name of the topic that you want to add.

Ⓐ As you type, News displays topics that match.

7 When you see the topic that you want, tap it.

Ⓑ News adds the topic to the My News page.

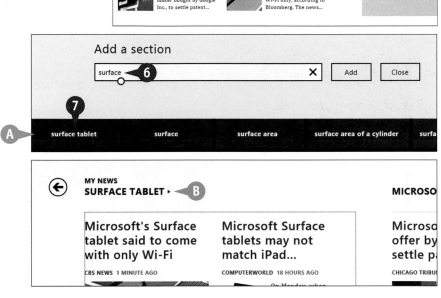

Can I see news that focuses on a particular country?
Yes. By default, the News app displays news from the country that you have defined in Windows 8's regional settings. To see news from another country instead, swipe left from the right edge of the screen to display the Charms menu, tap **Settings** to open the News app's Settings pane, and then tap **Settings**. Use the **Display content from** list to select the country whose news you want to view.

Track a Stock

Y‌ou can use the Finance app to read the latest financial news stories, see the latest financial data, and create a list of stocks to track.

The Finance app combines a wide variety of financial information in a single place. The Finance app's main page — called *Today* — displays financial news, Dow statistics, NASDAQ information, other index values, major stock activity, bond prices, interest rates, and more. You can also use the Finance app to create a list — called a *watchlist* — of the stocks that you want to track.

Track a Stock

1 On the Start screen, tap **Finance**.

The Finance app appears.

A On the Today page, you can swipe left and right to see the latest financial news and data.

2 Swipe down from the top of the screen.

The application bar appears.

3 Tap **Watchlist**.

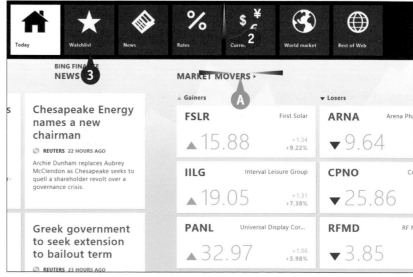

The Watchlist page appears.

4 Tap ⊕.

Note: You can also swipe up from the bottom edge of the screen and tap **Add**.

The Add to Watchlist screen appears.

5 Type the stock symbol or name of the stock that you want to add.

B As you type, Finance displays stocks that match.

6 When you see the stock that you want, tap it.

C Finance adds the stock to the Watchlist page.

Note: Your watchlist also appears on the Today page.

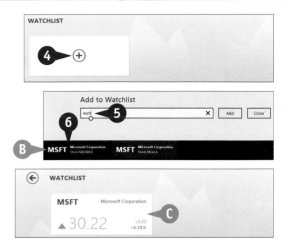

TIP

Is there a way to keep my watchlist on-screen so that I can monitor it?

Yes, there are a couple of ways that you can do this. If you frequently refer to the Start screen, you can pin your watchlist so that it appears as a Start screen tile. In the Finance app, swipe up from the bottom of the screen, tap **Pin Watchlist**, and then tap **Pin to Start**. Alternatively, snap Finance to the edge of the screen. In Finance, swipe down from the top edge of the screen until you see the app window, swipe the window to the left or right edge of the screen, and then release.

Follow Your Favorite Teams

You can use the Sports app to catch up on all your sports news.

The Sports app combines a wide variety of sports news and information in a single place. The Sports app's main page — called *Today* — displays the top story of the day, other sports news, the day's schedule of upcoming games, and the latest scores from those games. You can also use the Sports app to create a list — called *Favorite Teams* — of the teams that you want to follow.

Follow Your Favorite Teams

1 On the Start screen, tap **Sports**.

The Sports app appears.

A On the Today page, you can swipe left and right to see the latest sports news, schedules, and scores.

2 Swipe down from the top of the screen.

The application bar appears.

3 Tap **Favorite Teams**.

The Favorite Teams page appears.

④ Tap ⊕.

Note: You can also swipe up from the bottom edge of the screen and tap **Add**.

The Add to Favorite Teams screen appears.

⑤ Type the name of the team that you want to add.

Ⓑ As you type, Sports displays teams that match.

⑥ When you see the team that you want, tap it.

Ⓒ Sports adds the team to the Favorite Teams page.

⑦ Repeat steps **5** and **6** for every other team that you want to follow.

⑧ Tap **Close**.

You can now see news, schedules, and stats by tapping a team on the Favorite Teams screen.

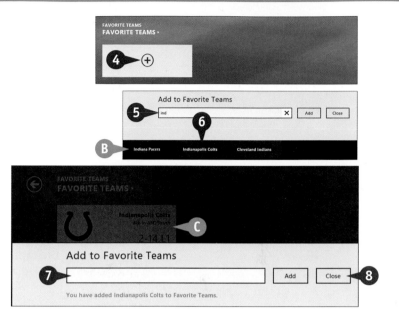

TIP

Can I see more information about a particular sport?

Yes, the Sports app offers detailed information on a number of sports leagues, including the National Football League, the National Basketball Association, Major League Baseball, and the National Hockey League. For each league, you see the latest news stories, a schedule of upcoming games, recent results, current standings, player statistics, and more.

To select a league, swipe down from the top edge of the screen and then tap a league in the application bar.

CHAPTER 9

Configuring Your Tablet

Windows 8 comes with many features designed to help you configure your tablet. In this chapter, you learn how to use the Mobility Center, improve battery life, configure the touch keyboard, add a second monitor, and more.

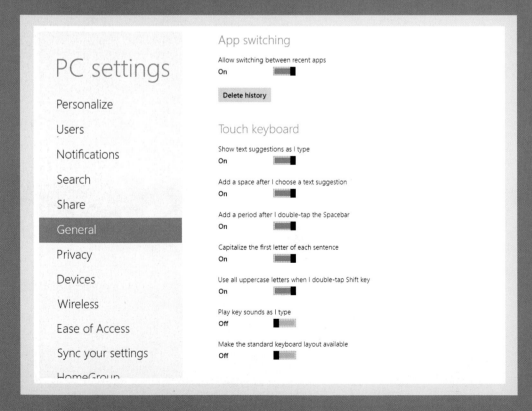

Display Mobility Settings

You can quickly see and change certain tablet settings by displaying the Windows Mobility Center feature.

The Windows Mobility Center enables you to adjust the display brightness, set or mute the volume, monitor battery power, and choose a power plan. You can also use the Windows Mobility Center to rotate the screen of a tablet PC, connect an external display, and more.

Display Mobility Settings

1 Swipe left from the right edge of the screen.

The Charms menu appears.

2 Tap **Search**.

The Search pane appears.

3 Tap **Settings**.

4 Type **mobility**.

Windows 8 displays the "mobility" search results.

5 Tap **Windows Mobility Center**.

The Windows Mobility Center window appears.

Ⓐ The top part of each section tells you the current status of the setting.

Ⓑ The middle part of each section offers a control that you can use to change the setting.

Ⓒ The bottom part of each section tells you the name of the setting.

6 When you are done, tap the Close button (❌) to shut down the Mobility Center.

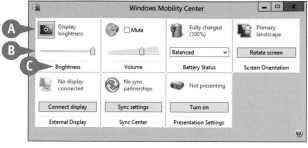

TIPS

Why can I not change some of the settings in the Mobility Center?

Not all tablets support the seven settings in the default Mobility Center. For example, only tablet PCs support the Screen Orientation setting. Similarly, you can use the External Display settings only if you have an external monitor attached to your tablet.

Is there a quicker way to open the Mobility Center?
Yes. Follow these steps:

1 Tap and hold the Power icon (🔲) in the taskbar's notification area.

2 Tap Windows Mobility Center.

The Mobility Center window appears.

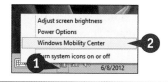

Display Power Options

You can use the Power Options window to choose a power plan for your tablet as well as other power-related features.

You can get the most out of your tablet battery by shutting down components when you are not using them. However, rather than shutting down components manually, the Power Options window enables you to choose a power plan that configures Windows 8 to shut down tablet components for you automatically. The Power Options window also enables you to configure other power-related features, many of which are covered in the next few sections of this chapter.

Display Power Options

Open the Power Options Window

1. Swipe left from the right edge of the screen.

   The Charms menu appears.

2. Tap **Search**.

   The Search pane appears.

3. Tap **Settings**.

4. Type **power**.

   Windows 8 displays the "power" search results.

5. Tap **Power Options**.

The Power Options window appears.

Choose a Power Plan

1 Tap here to display more power plans.

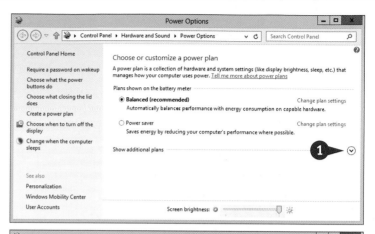

2 Tap the power plan that you want to use (○ changes to ⦿).

Windows 8 now manages your tablet hardware according to the new power plan settings.

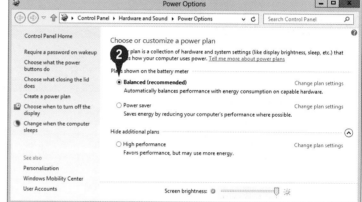

TIPS

Is there a quicker way to open the Power Options window or choose a power plan?

Yes. Follow these steps:

1 Tap 🔋.

2 Tap the power plan that you want (○ changes to ⦿).

A To open the Power Options window, tap **More power options**.

Which power plan should I use?

The power plan that you choose depends on how you are using your tablet. If you are on battery power, choose the Power Saver plan to maximize battery life. If you are running on AC power, choose the High Performance plan to reduce the frequency with which Windows 8 shuts down the tablet components. If you do not want to bother switching plans, choose the Balanced plan.

Define an Action for the Tablet Power Button

You can get easy access to the Windows 8 power-down modes — Shut Down, Sleep, and Hibernate — by configuring your tablet's power button.

Windows 8 enables you to configure three "power buttons": the on/off button, the sleep button, and closing the lid. Of these three, your tablet likely comes with only an on/off button, but you might have the other power buttons if you are using a tablet PC. When you activate these buttons, they put your system into Shut Down, Sleep, or Hibernate mode, depending on your configuration.

Define an Action for the Tablet Power Button

1 Open the Power Options window.

Note: See the preceding section, "Display Power Options," for details.

2 Tap **Choose what the power buttons do**.

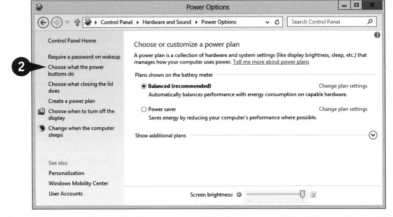

The System Settings window appears.

3 Under **On battery**, tap the **When I press the power button** ⌄ and then tap a power mode.

4 Under **Plugged in**, tap the **When I press the power button** ⌄ and then tap a power mode.

Note: If your tablet does not have a sleep button or a lid, skip to step **8**.

5 Under **On battery**, tap the **When I press the sleep button** ☑ and then tap a power mode.

6 Under **On battery**, tap the **When I close the lid** ☑ and then tap a power mode.

7 Repeat steps **5** and **6** for the **Plugged in** options.

8 Tap **Save changes**.

Windows 8 puts the new power button settings into effect.

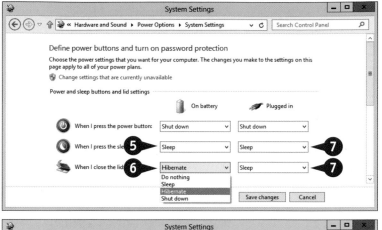

TIPS

What are the differences between the power modes?

- **Shut down:** Windows 8 closes your open programs and shuts off every component. The tablet uses no power when shut down.

- **Sleep:** Windows 8 saves all open programs and documents to memory and turns off everything but the memory chips. The tablet uses a bit of power (for the memory chips) when off. When you restart, Windows 8 restores your desktop as it was in just a few seconds.

- **Hibernate:** Same as sleep, except that Windows 8 saves your open programs and documents to a file and then shuts down. The tablet uses no power when it is off.

What do I do if I do not have a sleep button on my tablet?

Most tablets and many tablet PCs do not come with a separate sleep button. On these devices, you usually simulate the sleep button by quickly pressing and releasing the power button.

Adjust Screen Brightness

You can extend the battery life of your tablet by turning down the screen brightness. Your tablet screen uses a lot of power, so turning down the brightness also reduces battery drain.

On the other hand, if you have trouble seeing the data on your tablet screen, you can often fix the problem by *increasing* the screen brightness. This is not a problem when your tablet is running on AC power. However, you should not use full screen brightness for very long when your tablet is running on its battery because a bright screen uses a lot of power.

Adjust Screen Brightness

1 Open the Power Options window.

Note: See the section "Display Power Options" for details.

A On many tablets, you can tap and drag this slider to set the screen brightness for all power plans.

2 Under the power plan that you want to customize, tap **Change plan settings**.

The Edit Plan Settings window appears.

3 Tap and drag this slider to set the screen brightness while on battery power.

4 Tap and drag this slider to set the screen brightness while your tablet is plugged in.

5 Tap **Save changes**.

Windows 8 puts the new brightness settings into effect.

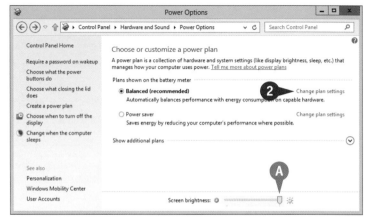

Monitor Battery Life

You can use the Power icon (🔋) in the taskbar's notification area to monitor your tablet's remaining battery power. When the battery is at maximum charge, the icon shows as all white. As the battery charge falls, the amount of white in the icon also falls.

You can also position your stylus cursor over the icon or tap the icon to see a tooltip that shows you the current battery level.

Monitor Battery Life

① Remove the power cord from your tablet to switch to battery power.

The Power icon changes from 🔋 to 🔋.

② Tap 🔋.

Ⓐ The current battery level is shown here.

Set a Battery Alarm to Avoid Running Out of Power

You can configure Windows 8 to warn you when your tablet battery level is running low so that your tablet does not shut down on you unexpectedly. This warning gives you enough time to save your work and possibly shut down the tablet until you can recharge it.

Windows 8 enables you to determine what the *low battery level* is, which is the percentage of remaining battery life that triggers the alarm. The default low battery level is ten percent. If you opt for a lower value, you can also configure Windows 8 to automatically go to sleep or shut down when the low battery level is reached.

Set a Battery Alarm to Avoid Running Out of Power

1 Open the Power Options window.

Note: See the section "Display Power Options" for details.

2 Beside your current power plan, tap **Change plan settings.**

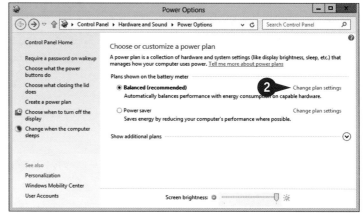

The Edit Plan Settings window appears.

3 Tap **Change advanced power settings**.

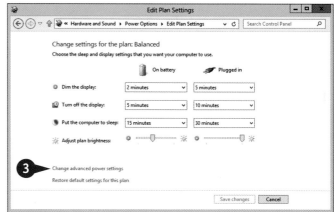

The Power Options dialog box appears.

4 Tap **+** to open the **Battery** branch.

5 Tap **+** to open **Low battery level**.

6 Tap **On battery**.

7 Type the percentage at which the low battery alarm is triggered.

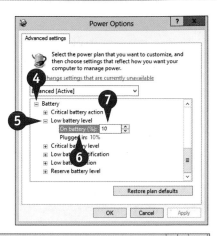

8 In the **Low battery notification** branch, tap **On battery** and tap **On**.

9 In the **Low battery action** branch, tap **On battery** and tap the action that you want Windows 8 to take at the low battery level.

10 Tap **OK**.

You are returned to the Edit Plan Settings window.

11 Tap **Save changes**.

Windows 8 will now display the battery alarm and trigger the low battery action according to your new settings.

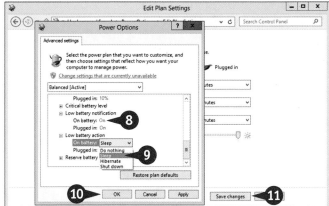

TIPS

Can I set the low battery options for other power plans?
Yes, you can set options for all three power plans: Balanced, High Performance, and Power Saver. Display the Power Options dialog box and then tap **Change plan settings** beside the power plan that you want to customize. Follow steps **3** to **11** in this section to set the low battery options for the plan.

Can I get a second low battery warning?
Yes. Windows 8 also supports a *critical battery level,* which is triggered when your battery becomes dangerously low — the default level is five percent. When this level is triggered, Windows 8 immediately puts the tablet into Hibernate mode. To change this, follow steps **1** to **4** in this section, open the **Critical battery action** branch, tap **On battery**, and tap the action that you want. You can also open the **Critical battery level** branch to specify the critical level.

Create a Custom Power Plan to Improve Battery Life

When you use a tablet on battery power, you always have to choose between increased battery life and tablet performance. For example, to increase battery life, Windows 8 shuts down components, such as the display and the hard disk after a short time.

You may find that none of the predefined power plans offers the blend of battery life and performance that is exactly right for you. If so, you can create a custom plan that suits the way you work, improving your tablet's battery life or increasing your productivity.

Create a Custom Power Plan to Improve Battery Life

1 Open the Power Options window.

Note: See the section "Display Power Options" for details.

2 Tap **Create a power plan**.

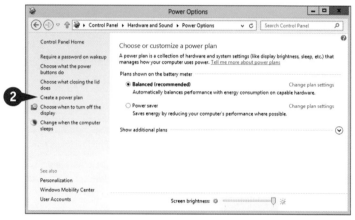

The Create a Power Plan window appears.

3 Tap a predefined power plan to use as a starting point option (○ changes to ◉).

4 Type a name for your plan in the **Plan name** text box.

5 Tap **Next**.

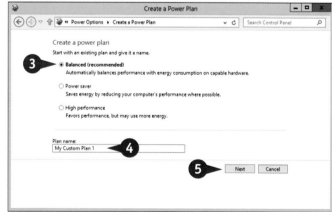

The Edit Plan Settings window appears.

6 Under **On battery**, use the lists to choose the idle intervals after which Windows 8 dims and turns off the display and puts the tablet to sleep while running on battery power.

7 Use the **Adjust plan brightness** slider to set the screen brightness while on battery power.

8 Repeat steps **6** and **7** under **Plugged in** to configure the settings while running on AC power.

9 Tap **Create**.

A The Power Options window appears with your custom plan displayed and selected.

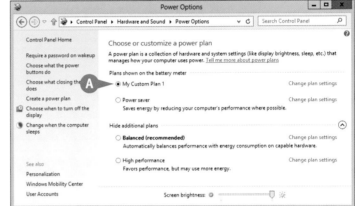

TIPS

Are there other options I can configure for my custom power plan?

To configure more advanced power options, such as when your hard disk powers down, open the Power Options window, tap **Change plan settings** beside your custom plan, and then tap **Change advanced power settings**. In the Power Options dialog box, use the branches such as **Hard disk**, **Sleep**, and **Processor power management** to set the idle intervals. Tap **OK** and then tap **Save changes**.

How can I remove a custom power plan that I no longer use?

To remove the custom plan, first change to a different plan by displaying the Power Options window and then tapping another plan. Beside your custom plan, tap **Change plan settings**, and then tap **Delete this plan**. When Windows 8 asks you to confirm, tap **OK**.

Configure the Touch Keyboard

The touch keyboard offers a number of features that make it easier to use. For example, the touch keyboard automatically adds a period and space when you double-tap the spacebar, and it automatically capitalizes the first letter of each sentence. However, the touch keyboard also has some features that you might not like — such as the noise it makes each time you tap a key.

You can use the PC Settings app to turn on the touch keyboard features that you like and turn off the features that you do not like.

Configure the Touch Keyboard

1 Swipe left from the right edge of the screen.

The Charms menu appears.

2 Tap **Settings**.

The Settings pane appears.

3 Tap **Change PC settings**.

The PC Settings app appears.

4 Tap **General**.

5 Under **Touch Keyboard**, tap each option **On** or **Off**, according to your preferences.

Windows 8 applies your new settings to the touch keyboard.

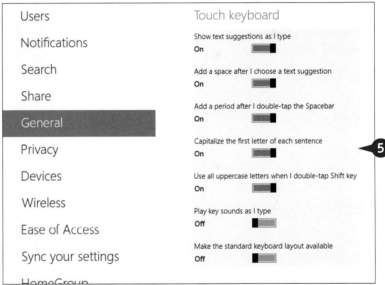

TIP

What is the standard keyboard layout?

If you tap the **Make the standard keyboard layout available** option to **On** in step **5** of this section, the next time that you use the keyboard, tap ⌨ and then tap ⊞. This presents a keyboard with all the keys that you see on a normal keyboard, including ⊞, Alt, Del, and Caps lock.

Configure Your Tablet to Work with a Second Monitor

You can improve your productivity and efficiency by using a second monitor. To work with an external monitor, your tablet must have a video output port, such as VGA, DVI, or HDMI. If you do not have such a port, check with the manufacturer to see if an adapter is available that enables your tablet to connect with an external monitor.

After you have connected your tablet and the external monitor, you then need to configure Windows 8 to extend the Start screen to both the tablet screen and the external monitor.

Configure Your Tablet to Work with a Second Monitor

Extend to the External Monitor

1. Connect the second monitor to your tablet.

2. Swipe left from the right edge of the screen.

   The Charms menu appears.

3. Tap **Devices**.

The Devices pane appears.

4. Tap **Second screen**.

The Second Screen pane appears.

5 Tap **Extend**.

Windows 8 connects to the second monitor and uses it to display the Desktop app.

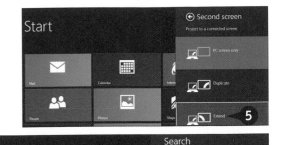

Set the Main Display

1 Swipe left from the right edge of the screen and then tap **Settings**.

The Settings search pane appears.

2 Type **resolution**.

Windows 8 displays the "resolution" search results.

3 Tap **Adjust screen resolution**.

The Screen Resolution dialog box appears on the desktop.

4 Tap the monitor that you want to set as the main display.

5 Tap the **Make this my main display** check box (☐ changes to ☑).

6 Tap **OK**.

Windows 8 uses the monitor that you selected as your main display.

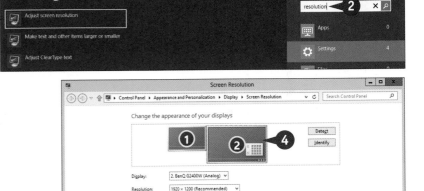

TIPS

Why does my cursor stop at the right edge of the left screen?

Ideally, you should be able to move your cursor continuously from the left monitor to the right monitor. If you find that the cursor stops at the right edge of your left monitor, it means that you need to exchange the icons of the left and right monitors. To do that, tap and drag the left monitor icon to the right of the other monitor icon (or vice versa).

I no longer need to use an external monitor. How do I configure Windows 8 to stop using it?

Follow steps **1** to **4** in this section to open the Second Screen pane and then tap **PC screen only**. You can also usually revert to using just the tablet screen by disconnecting the monitor from your tablet.

Calibrate the Screen for Accurate Tapping

Y ou have seen that you can use your finger or a digital stylus in the same way that you would use a mouse. That is, you can tap an object to select it, tap and drag an object to move it, and so on. However, the usefulness of this feature declines if your tapping is not calibrated to your tablet screen. This can cause taps and double-taps to occur in places that are slightly off where you intended them to occur. To prevent this, you need to calibrate your taps.

Calibrate the Screen for Accurate Tapping

1 Swipe left from the right edge of the screen and then tap **Search**.

The Search pane appears.

2 Tap **Settings**.

3 Type **calibrate**.

Windows 8 displays the "calibrate" search results.

4 Tap **Calibrate the screen for pen or touch input**.

The Tablet PC Settings dialog box appears.

5 Tap **Calibrate**.

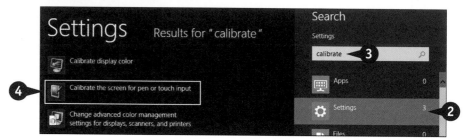

Windows 8 asks what type of screen you want to calibrate.

6 Tap **Touch input**.

Ⓐ If you use a digital stylus, tap **Pen input** instead.

Note: If you see the User Account Control dialog box, tap **Yes** or enter your Windows 8 administrator credentials.

The calibration window appears.

7 Tap the middle of the crosshair each time that it appears on your screen.

When the calibration is complete, the Digitizer Calibration Tool dialog box appears.

8 Tap **Yes**.

You are returned to the Tablet PC Settings dialog box.

9 Tap **OK**.

Your tablet screen is now calibrated.

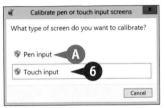

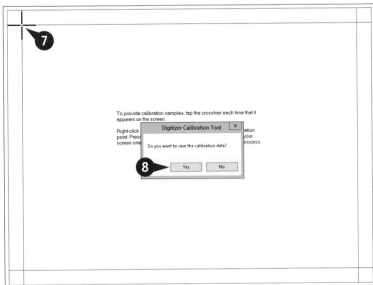

TIP

How do I turn off the circles that Windows 8 displays when I tap the screen?
When you tap the screen, Windows 8 displays a circle at the tap position. If you find this kind of visual feedback distracting, you can turn it off. Follow steps **1** to **4** in this section to open the Tablet PC Settings dialog box, tap the **Other** tab, tap **Go to Pen and Touch**, tap the **Touch** tab, and then tap the **Show visual feedback when touching the screen** check box (☑ changes to ☐). Tap **OK**.

CHAPTER 10

Creating and Editing Documents

To get productive with Windows 8, you need to know how to work with documents. In this chapter, you learn what documents are, and you learn how to create, save, open, edit, and print them.

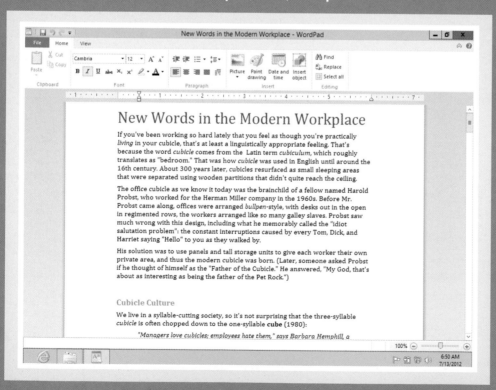

Understanding Documents

Documents are files that you create or edit yourself. The four examples shown here are the basic document types that you can create using the programs that come with Windows 8.

A Text Document

A *text document* is one that includes only the characters that you see on a computer keyboard, plus a few others; see the "Insert Special Symbols" section in this chapter. A text document contains no special formatting, such as colored text or bold formatting, although you can change the font. In Windows 8, you normally use the Notepad program to create text documents, although you can also use WordPad.

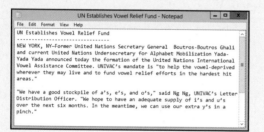

A Word-Processing Document

A *word-processing document* contains text and other symbols, but you can format those characters to improve the look of the document. For example, you can change the size, color, and typeface, and you can make words bold or italic. In Windows 8, you use the WordPad program to create word-processing documents.

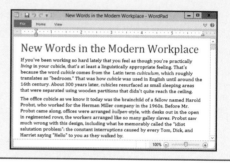

A Drawing

A *drawing* in this context is a digital image that you create using special tools that make lines, boxes, polygons, special effects, and free-form shapes. In Windows 8, you can use the Paint program to create drawings.

An E-mail Message

An *e-mail message* is a document that you send to another person via the Internet. Most e-mail messages use plain text, but some programs support formatted text, images, and other effects. In Windows 8, you can create and send e-mail messages using the Mail app, which is covered in Chapter 5, "Sending E-mail and Messages."

Create a Document

When you are ready to create something using Windows 8, in most cases, you begin by launching a program and then using that program to create a new document to hold your work.

Many Windows 8 programs, such as WordPad and Paint, create a new document for you automatically when you begin the program. However, you can also use these programs to create other new documents after you have started the programs.

Create a Document

1 Start the program that you want to work with.

2 Tap **File**.

3 Tap **New**.

A If the program supports more than one type of file, the program asks which type you want to create.

Note: Some programs display a dialog box with a list of document types.

4 Tap the document type that you want.

The program creates the new document.

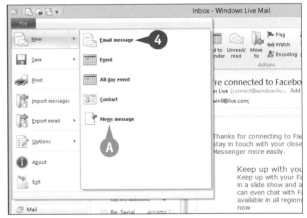

Save a Document

After you create a document and make any changes to it, you can save the document to preserve your work.

When you work on a document, Windows 8 stores the changes in your tablet's memory. However, Windows erases the contents of your memory each time that you shut down or restart the tablet. This means that the changes you have made to your document are lost when you turn off or restart your tablet. Saving the document preserves your changes on your tablet's hard drive.

Save a Document

1 Tap **File**.

2 Tap **Save**.

Note: In most programs, you can also tap the Save button (⊞).

Note: If you saved the document previously, your changes are now preserved. You do not need to follow the rest of the steps in this section.

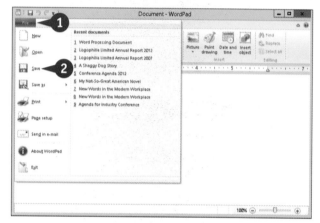

If this is a new document that you have never saved before, the Save As dialog box appears.

3 Tap **Documents**.

Note: In most programs, the Documents folder is selected automatically when you save a document.

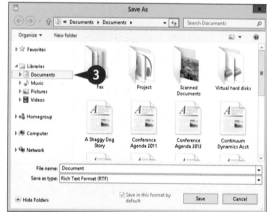

Ⓐ Windows 8 opens the Documents folder.

④ Tap in the **File name** text box and type the name that you want to use for the document.

Note: The name that you type can be up to 255 characters long, but it cannot include the following characters: < > , ? : " \ *.

⑤ Tap **Save**.

Ⓑ The filename that you chose appears in the program's title bar.

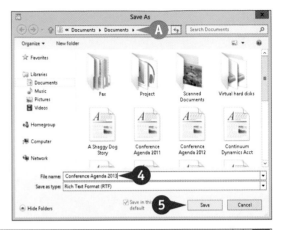

Can I create different types of documents in a program?

Yes, in most programs. With WordPad, for example, you can create both word-processing documents and text documents. However, Notepad supports only text documents. If the program supports multiple document types, the Save As dialog box includes a drop-down list named *Save as type*, or something similar. Use that list to choose the document type that you want.

Do I have to save all my files to the Documents folder?

No, not necessarily. The Documents folder is a convenient place because having everything in one location makes it easier to find your files. However, if you have several related files, you can create a subfolder within Documents and use it to store the related files. In the Save As dialog box, tap **New folder**, type the name of the folder, press Enter, double-tap the new folder, and then follow steps **4** and **5** in this section.

Open a Document

To work with a document that you have saved in the past, you need to open the document in the program that you used to create it.

When you save a document, you save its contents to your tablet's hard disk, and those contents are stored in a separate file. When you open the document using the same application that you used to save it, Windows loads the file's contents into memory and displays the document in the application. You can then view and edit the document as needed.

Open a Document

1 Start the program that you want to work with.

2 Tap **File**.

A If you see the document that you want in a list of the most recently used documents on the File menu, tap the name to open it. You can skip the rest of the steps in this section.

3 Tap **Open**.

Note: In most programs, you can also tap the **Open** button ().

The Open dialog box appears.

4 Tap **Documents**.

Note: In most programs, the Documents folder is selected automatically when you open a document.

B If you want to open a document from a different folder, tap here, tap your username, and then double-tap the folder.

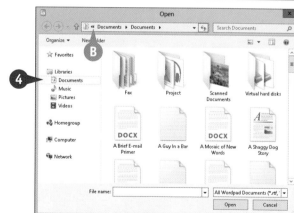

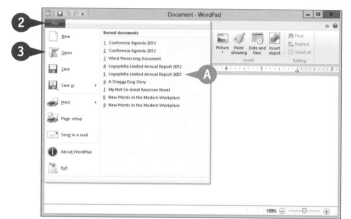

C Windows 8 opens the Documents folder.

5 Tap the document name.

6 Tap **Open**.

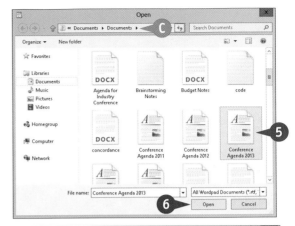

D The document appears in the program window.

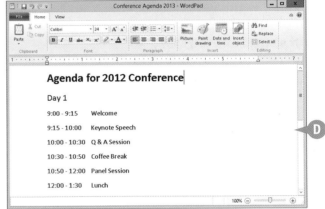

TIPS

Is there a more direct way to open a document than what is shown in this section?

Yes, there is. You do not always need to open the program first. Instead, open the folder that contains the document and then double-tap the document. Windows 8 automatically launches the program and opens the document.

Is there a quick way to locate a document?

Yes, Windows 8 offers a file search feature, which is handy if your Documents folder contains many files. On the Start screen, swipe from the right edge of your tablet screen, tap **Search**, and then tap **Files**. Type some or all of the document's filename and then double-tap the document in the search results.

Edit the Document Text

When you work with a character-based file, such as a text or word-processing document or an e-mail message, it is rare that any text you enter into a document is perfect the first time through. It is far more likely that the text contains errors that require correcting or words, sentences, or paragraphs that appear in the wrong place.

To get your document text the way you want it, you need to know how to edit text, including deleting characters, selecting the text that you want to work with, and copying and moving text.

Edit the Document Text

Delete Characters

1 Tap immediately to the right of the first character that you want to delete.

A The cursor appears after the character.

2 Tap ⌫ until you have deleted all the characters that you want.

Note: If you make a mistake, immediately tap the Undo button (⟲).

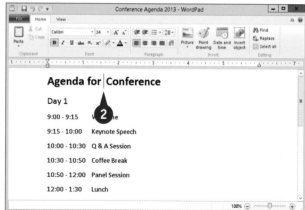

Select Text for Editing

1 Tap and drag across the text that you want to select.

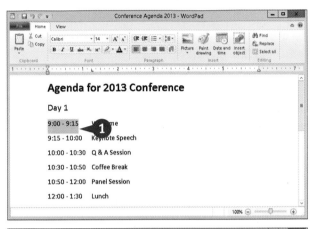

2 Release your finger or stylus.

B The program highlights the selected text.

TIP

Are there any shortcut methods that I can use to select text in WordPad?

Yes. Here are the most useful ones:

- Tap in the white space to the left of a line to select the line.
- Double-tap a word to select it.
- Triple-tap inside a paragraph to select it.
- Use the on-screen keyboard to press **Ctrl**+**A** to select the entire document. In many apps, you can also tap the **Select all** command.

continued ▶

Edit the Document Text (continued)

After you select some text, you can then copy or move the text to another location in your document.

Copying text is often a useful way to save work. For example, if you want to use the same passage of text elsewhere in a document, you can copy and paste it instead of typing it again from scratch. If you need just a similar passage in another part of the document, you can edit the copy as needed.

If a passage of text is in the wrong position within a document, you can fix that by moving it to the correct location.

Edit the Document Text (continued)

Copy Text

1 Select the text that you want to copy.

2 Tap **Copy** (⬚).

Note: You can also tap and hold the selection and then tap **Copy**.

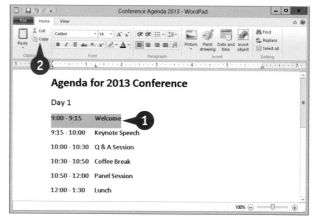

3 Tap inside the document at the position where you want the copy of the text to appear.

The cursor appears in the position that you tapped.

4 Tap **Paste** (⬚).

Note: You can also tap and hold at the location and then tap **Paste**.

A The program inserts a copy of the selected text at the cursor position.

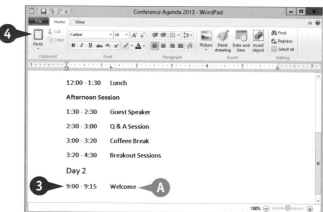

Move Text

1 Select the text that you want to move.

2 Tap **Cut** (✂).

Note: You can also tap and hold the selection and then tap **Cut**.

The program removes the text from the document.

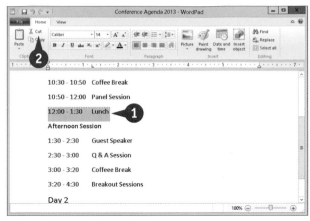

3 Tap inside the document at the position where you want to move the text.

The cursor appears at the position that you tapped.

4 Tap 📋.

Note: You can also tap and hold at the location and then tap **Paste**.

B The program inserts the text at the cursor position.

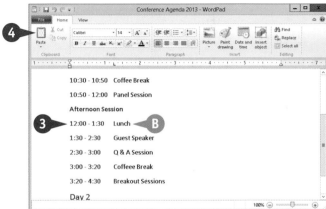

TIP

If I have the on-screen keyboard displayed, are there any shortcuts that I can use to copy and move text?

Yes, there are several shortcuts that you can use to copy, cut, and paste text:

- Tap Ctrl+C to copy the selected text.
- Tap Ctrl+X to cut the selected text.
- Tap Ctrl+V to paste the copied or cut text.
- Tap Ctrl+Z to undo your most recent cut or paste operation.

Change the Font Formatting

When you work in a word-processing document, you can add visual appeal by changing the font formatting.

The font formatting includes attributes such as the typeface, style, size, or special effects. A *typeface* — also called a *font* — is a distinctive character design of text. The *type style* refers to formatting applied to the text, such as **bold** or *italics*. The *type size* refers to the height of each character, which is measured in *points:* 72 points equal one inch. *Special effects* are styles that change the appearance of the text. The most common examples are <u>underline</u> and ~~strikethrough~~.

Change the Font Formatting

1 Select the text that you want to format.

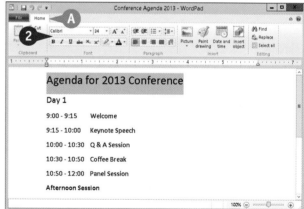

2 Display the font options.

A In WordPad, you display the font options by tapping the **Home** tab.

Note: In many other programs, you display the font options by tapping **Format** in the menu bar and then tapping the **Font** command.

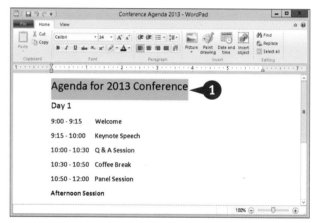

3 In the Font list, tap ☑ and then tap the typeface that you want.

4 In the Size list, tap ☑ and then tap the type size that you want.

5 For bold text, tap **B**.

6 For italics, tap *I*.

7 For underlining, tap U.

8 For color, tap the Font Color ☑ and then tap a color.

B The program applies the font formatting to the selected text.

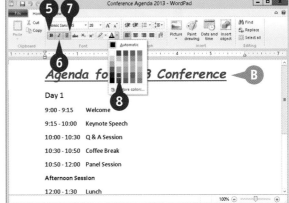

TIP

How can I make the best use of fonts in my documents?

- Do not use many different typefaces in a single document. Stick to one or at most two typefaces to avoid the "ransom-note look."
- Avoid overly decorative typefaces because they are often difficult to read.
- Use bold only for document titles, subtitles, and headings.
- Use italics only to emphasize words and phrases or for the titles of books and magazines.
- Use larger type sizes only for document titles, subtitles, and, possibly, the headings.
- If you change the text color, be sure to leave enough contrast between the text and the background. In general, dark text on a light background is the easiest to read.

Find Text

In large documents, when you need to find specific text, you can save a lot of time by using the program's Find feature.

In short documents that contain only a few dozen or a couple hundred words, it is usually not difficult to find a specific word or phrase. However, many documents contain hundreds or even thousands of words, so finding a word or phrase becomes much more difficult and time-consuming. You can work around this problem by using the Find feature, which searches the entire document very quickly.

Find Text

1 Tap **Find** (🔍).

Note: In many programs, you run the Find command by tapping **Edit** in the menu bar and then tapping the **Find** command or by pressing `Ctrl`+`F` on the on-screen keyboard.

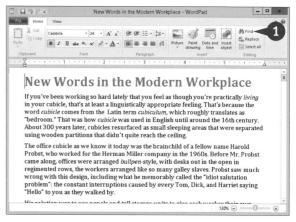

The Find dialog box appears.

2 Tap in the **Find what** text box and type the text that you want to find.

3 Tap **Find Next**.

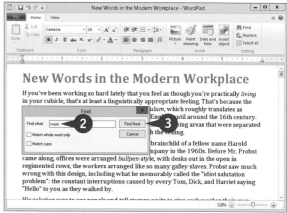

A The program selects the next instance of the search text.

Note: If the search text does not exist in the document, the program displays a dialog box to let you know.

4 If the selected instance is not the one that you want, tap **Find Next** until the program finds the correct instance.

5 Tap ✕ to close the dialog box.

B The program leaves the found text selected.

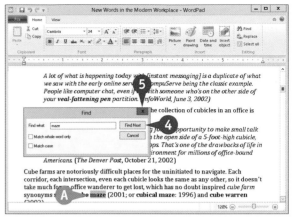

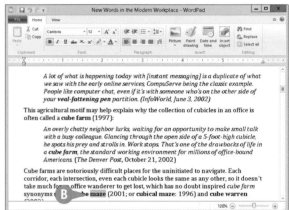

TIPS

When I search for a small word such as *the*, the program matches it in larger words such as *theme* and *bother*. How can I avoid this?

In the Find dialog box, tap **Match whole word only** (□ changes to ✔). This tells the program to match the search text only if it is a word on its own and not part of another word.

When I search for a name such as *Bill*, the program also matches the non-name *bill*. Is there a way to fix this?

In the Find dialog box, tap **Match case** (□ changes to ✔). This tells the program to match the search text only if it has the same mix of uppercase and lowercase letters that you specify in the **Find what** text box. If you type **Bill**, for example, the program matches only *Bill* and not *bill*.

Replace Text

Do you need to replace a word or part of a word with some other text? If you have several instances of one word to replace, you can save time, do a more accurate job, and make the replacement more easily if you let the program's Replace feature replace the word for you.

Most programs that work with text — including Windows 8's WordPad and Notepad programs — have the Replace feature.

Replace Text

1 Tap **Replace** (▦).

Note: In many programs, you run the Replace command by tapping **Edit** in the menu bar and then tapping the **Replace** command or by pressing Ctrl + H in the on-screen keyboard.

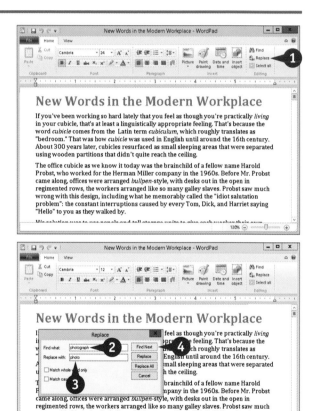

The Replace dialog box appears.

2 In the **Find what** text box, type the text that you want to find.

3 Tap in the **Replace with** text box and type the text that you want to use as the replacement.

4 Tap **Find Next**.

Ⓐ The program selects the next instance of the search text.

Note: If the search text does not exist in the document, the program displays a dialog box to let you know.

⑤ If the selected instance is not the one that you want, tap **Find Next** until the program finds the correct instance.

⑥ Tap **Replace**.

Ⓑ The program replaces the selected text with the replacement text.

Ⓒ The program selects the next instance of the search text.

⑦ Repeat steps **5** and **6** until you have replaced all the instances that you want to.

⑧ Tap the [×] to close the Replace dialog box.

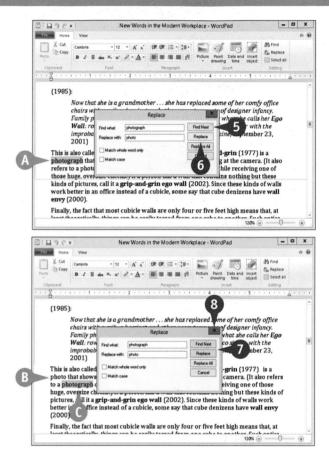

TIP

Is there a faster way to replace every instance of the search text with the replacement text?
Yes. In the Replace dialog box, tap **Replace all**. This tells the program to replace every instance of the search text with the replacement text. However, you should exercise some caution with this feature because it may make some replacements that you did not intend. Tap **Find Next** a few times to make sure that the matches are correct. Also, consider tapping the **Match whole word only** and **Match case** check boxes (☐ changes to ☑), as described in the "Find Text" section of this chapter.

Insert Special Symbols

You can make your documents more readable and more useful by inserting special symbols that are not available via the on-screen keyboard.

The on-screen keyboard is home to a large number of letters, numbers, and symbols. However, the keyboard is missing some useful characters. For example, it is missing the foreign characters in words such as café and Köln. These and many more symbols are available in Windows 8 in the Character Map program.

Insert Special Symbols

1 Swipe up from the bottom edge of the screen and then tap **All apps**.

2 Tap **Character Map**.

The Character Map window appears.

3 Tap the symbol that you want.

4 Tap **Select**.

Ⓐ Character Map adds the symbol to the Characters to Copy text box.

5 Tap **Copy**.

6 Tap ▨ after you choose all the characters that you want.

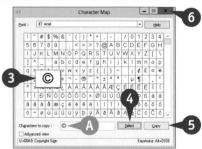

7 In your document, position the cursor where you want to insert the symbol.

8 Tap **Paste** (📋).

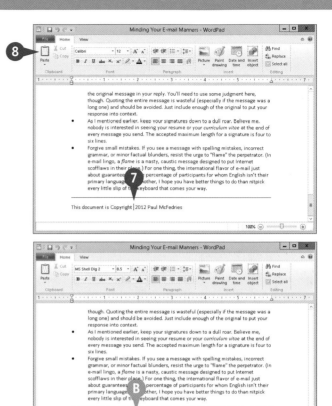

B The program inserts the symbol.

Are there even more symbols available?

Yes, there are dozens of extra symbols available in the Character Map program's Webdings and Wingdings typefaces. To see these symbols, tap the **Font** ⌄ and then tap either **Webdings** or **Wingdings**.

Is there another method that I can use to insert special symbols?

Yes, you can use the touch keyboard to insert symbols without using the Character Map program. In the touch keyboard, tap 🔲 to display the basic symbols and the numeric keypad. Tap and hold a symbol key. If the key supports extra symbols, they appear on the screen. Slide your finger to the symbol you want and then release to insert that symbol.

Make a Copy of a Document

When you need to create a document that is nearly identical to an existing document, instead of creating the new document from scratch, you can save time by making a copy of the existing document and then modifying the copy as needed.

For example, you might have a resume cover letter that you want to modify for a different job application. Or you may be creating a conference agenda for this year; it is likely to be similar to last year's agenda, so you can copy and update it.

Make a Copy of a Document

1 Start the program that you want to work with and open the original document.

2 Tap **File**.

3 Tap **Save as**.

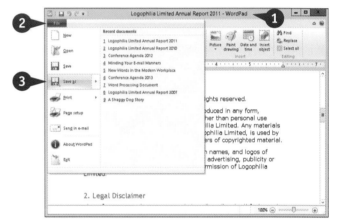

The Save As dialog box appears.

4 Tap **Documents**.

Note: In most programs, the Documents folder is selected automatically when you run the Save As command.

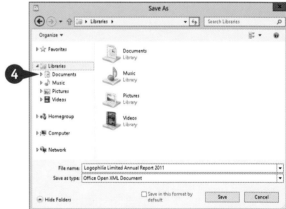

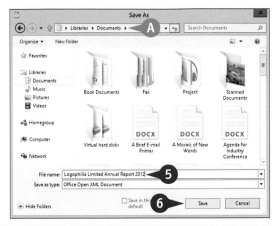

Ⓐ Windows 8 opens the Documents folder.

⑤ Tap in the **File name** text box and type the name that you want to use for the copy.

Note: The name that you type can be up to 255 characters long, but it cannot include the following characters: < > , ? : " \ *.

⑥ Tap **Save**.

The program closes the original document and opens the copy that you just created.

Ⓑ The filename that you chose appears in the program's title bar.

Print a Document

When you need a hard copy of your document, either for your files or to distribute to someone else, you can send the document to your printer.

Most applications that deal with documents also come with a Print command. When you run this command, the Print dialog box appears. You use the Print dialog box to choose the printer that you want to use as well as to specify how many copies you want to print. Many Print dialog boxes also enable you to see a preview of your document before you print it.

Print a Document

1 Turn on your printer.

2 Open the document that you want to print.

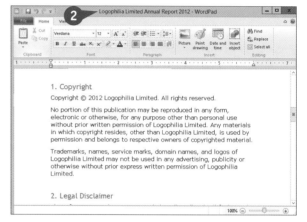

3 Tap **File**.

4 Tap **Print**.

Note: In many programs, you can select the Print command by pressing `Ctrl`+`P` or by tapping the **Print** button (🖶).

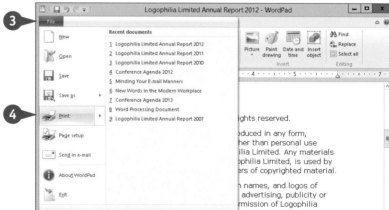

The Print dialog box appears.

Note: The layout of the Print dialog box varies from program to program. The WordPad version shown here is a typical example.

5 If you have more than one printer, tap the printer that you want to use.

Note: If you join a homegroup, as described in Chapter 12, any shared printers automatically appear in this list.

6 Use the **Number of copies** text box to specify the number of copies to print.

7 Tap **Print**.

Ⓐ Windows 8 prints the document. 🖶 appears in the taskbar's notification area while the document prints.

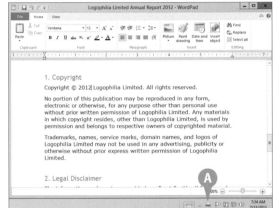

How do I print only part of a document?

Most programs enable you to use the following methods to print only part of the document:

• Print selected text: Select the text that you want to print. In the Print dialog box, tap **Selection** (○ changes to ⦿).

• Print a specific page: Place the cursor on the page that you want to print. In the Print dialog box, tap **Current Page** (○ changes to ⦿).

• Print a range of pages: In the Print dialog box, tap **Pages** (○ changes to ⦿). In the text box, type the first page number, a dash (–), and the last page number (for example, 1–5).

Can I preview my document before I print it?

Yes. It is a good idea to preview the document before printing it to ensure that the document layout looks the way you want. To preview the document in WordPad, tap **File**, tap the **Print** ▶, and then tap **Print preview**.

CHAPTER 11

Working with Files

This chapter shows you how to work with the files on your tablet.
These easy and efficient methods show you how to view, select, copy,
move, rename, and delete files, as well as how to restore accidentally
deleted files, compress and extract files, send a file to SkyDrive, and
share files with friends.

View Your Files

You can view the files that you create, as well as those stored on your hard drive that you download and copy to your tablet. If you want to open or work with those files, you first need to view them.

Windows 8 stores files on your hard drive using special storage areas called *folders*. A *folder* is a location on your hard drive that contains one or more related files. You can also store folders within folders, and these nested folders are known as *subfolders*. To view your files, you usually have to open one or more folders and subfolders.

View Your Files

1 On the Start screen, tap **Desktop**.

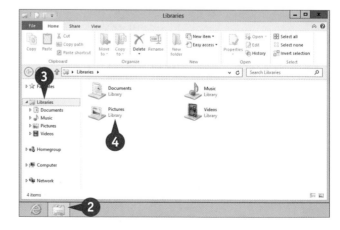

2 Tap the File Explorer button (📁).

File Explorer opens.

3 Tap **Libraries**.

The libraries appear.

4 Double-tap the folder containing the files that you want to view.

Windows 8 displays the contents of the folder, including subfolders.

5 If the files that you want to view are stored in a subfolder, double-tap the subfolder.

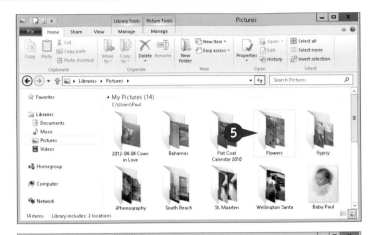

Windows 8 displays the contents of the subfolder.

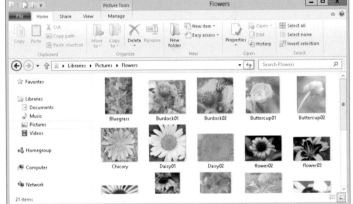

TIPS

How do I view the files that I have on a flash drive, memory card, or other media?

Insert the media into the appropriate drive or slot on your tablet. If you see the AutoPlay notification, tap it and then tap **Open folder to view files**. Otherwise, open File Explorer, tap **Computer** to display the Computer folder, and then double-tap the disk drive or device that contains the files you want to view. Windows 8 displays the contents of the media.

What is a file library?

In Windows 8, the four main document storage areas — Documents, Music, Pictures, and Videos — are set up as *libraries*, where each library consists of two or more folders. For example, the Documents library consists of your My Documents folder and the Public Documents folder. To add a folder to a library, open the folder, tap the **Home** tab, tap **Easy access**, tap **Include in library**, and then tap the library.

Select a File

Before you can do any work with one or more files, you first have to select the files so that Windows 8 knows exactly which ones you want to work with. You learn later in this chapter how to copy files to a different folder, how to move files to a new location, how to rename a file, and how to delete one or more files. Before you can perform any of these operations, you must first select the files.

Although you learn specifically about selecting files in this section, the technique for selecting folders is exactly the same.

Select a File

Select a Single File

1 Open the folder containing the file.

2 Tap the file.

The file is selected.

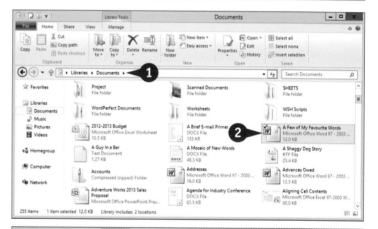

Select Multiple Files

1 Open the folder containing the files.

2 Tap the first file that you want to select.

3 Tap the check box for each of the other files that you want to select (☐ changes to ☑).

A For views that do not show the check box, tap the upper-left corner of the file icon.

Note: See the following section, "Change the File View," to learn more about File Explorer's views.

The files are selected.

Select a Group of Files

1 Open the folder containing the files.

2 Position your finger or the stylus slightly above and slightly to the left of the first file in the group.

3 Tap and drag down and to the right until all the files in the group are selected.

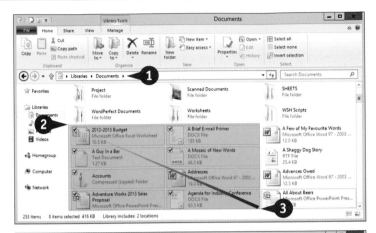

Select All the Files in a Folder

1 Open the folder containing the files.

2 Tap the **Home** tab.

3 Tap **Select all**.

B All the files in the folder are selected.

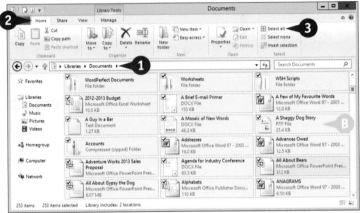

TIP

How do I deselect a file?

- To deselect a single file from a multiple-file selection, tap the check box of the file that you want to deselect (☑ changes to ☐).
- To deselect all the files from a group of selected files, either tap the **Home** tab and then tap **Select none** or tap an empty area within the folder.
- To reverse the selection — deselect the selected files and select the deselected files — tap the **Home** tab and then tap **Invert selection**.

Change the File View

You can configure how Windows 8 displays the files in a folder by changing the file view. This enables you to see larger or smaller icons or the details of each file.

Choose a view such as Small Icons to see more files in the folder window. Choose a view such as Large Icons or Extra Large Icons when you are viewing images to see thumbnail versions of each picture. If you want to see more information about the files, choose either the Tiles view or Details view.

Change the File View

1 Open the folder containing the files that you want to view.

2 Tap the **View** tab.

3 In the **Layout** section, tap ▾.

Windows 8 displays the Layout gallery.

4 Tap the view that you want.

Ⓐ File Explorer changes the file view — to Tiles, in this example.

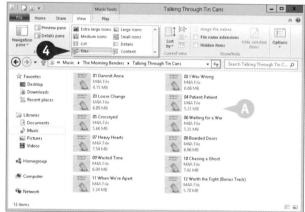

Preview a File

Windows 8 enables you to view the contents of some files without opening them. This makes it easier to select the file you want to work with because it means that you do not have to run an application to see the file's contents. Previewing the file is faster and uses fewer system resources.

Windows 8 can show previews of only certain types of files, such as text documents, rich text documents, web pages, images, and videos.

Preview a File

① Open the folder containing the file that you want to preview.

② Tap the **View** tab.

③ Tap **Preview pane**.

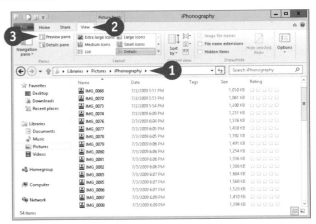

Ⓐ The Preview pane appears.

④ Tap the file that you want to preview.

Ⓑ The file's contents appear in the Preview pane.

Ⓒ You can tap and drag the left border of the Preview pane to change its size.

Ⓓ When you are finished with the Preview pane, tap **Preview pane** to close it.

Copy a File

You can make an exact copy of a file. This is useful if you want to back up an important file by making an extra copy on a flash drive, memory card, or other removable disk. Similarly, you might require a copy of a file if you want to send the copy on a disk to another person.

This section shows you how to copy a single file, but the steps also work if you select multiple files. You can also use these steps to copy a folder.

Copy a File

1 Open the folder containing the file that you want to copy.

2 Select the file.

3 Tap the **Home** tab.

4 Tap **Copy**.

Windows 8 places a copy of the file in a special memory location called the *clipboard*.

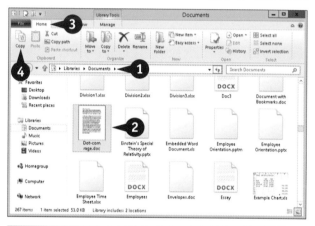

5 Open the location that you want to use to store the copy.

6 Tap the **Home** tab.

7 Tap **Paste**.

Ⓐ Windows 8 inserts a copy of the file in the location.

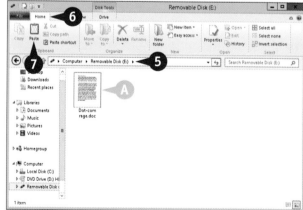

Move a File

When you need to store a file in a new location, the easiest way is to move the file from its current folder to another folder on your tablet's hard disk. When you save a file for the first time, you specify a folder on your tablet's hard disk in which to place it. This original location does not have to be permanent, of course.

This section shows you how to move a single file, but the steps also work if you select multiple files. You can also use these steps to move a folder.

Move a File

1 Open the folder containing the file that you want to move.

2 Select the file.

3 Tap the **Home** tab.

4 Tap **Cut**.

Windows 8 removes the file from the folder and places it in a special memory location called the *clipboard*.

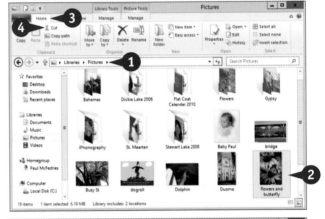

5 Tap the new location that you want to use for the file.

6 Tap the **Home** tab.

7 Tap **Paste**.

Ⓐ Windows 8 inserts the file in the new location.

Rename a File

You can change the name of a file, which is useful if its current name does not accurately describe the file's contents. By giving your document a descriptive name, you make it easier to find the file later.

Make sure that you rename only those documents that you have created yourself or that have been given to you by someone else. Do not rename any of the Windows 8 system files or any files associated with your programs, or your tablet may behave erratically — or even crash.

Rename a File

1 Open the folder that contains the file that you want to rename.

2 Tap the file.

3 Tap the **Home** tab.

Note: In addition to renaming files, you can also rename any folders that you created yourself.

4 Tap **Rename**.

A text box appears around the filename.

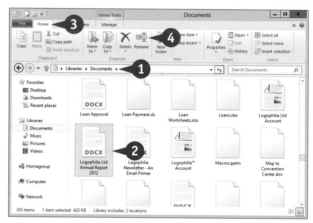

5 Type the new name that you want to use for the file.

Note: If you decide that you do not want to rename the file after all, tap Esc to cancel the operation.

Note: The name can be up to 255 characters long, but it cannot include the following characters: < > , ? : " \ *.

6 Tap an empty section of the folder.

The new name appears under the file's icon.

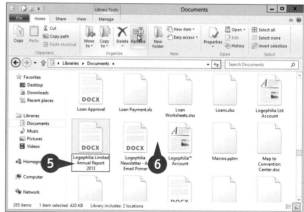

Create a New File

You can quickly create a new file directly within a file folder. This method is faster, and often more convenient, than running a program's New command, as explained in the "Create a Document" section in Chapter 10.

In Windows 8, you can create seven different types of files, the most important of which are a bitmap image (a drawing), a rich text document (a WordPad file), a text document (a Notepad file), and a compressed (zipped) folder, which combines multiple files in a single file, as described later in this chapter. You can also create a new folder.

Create a New File

1 Open the folder in which you want to create a file.

2 Tap the **Home** tab.

3 Tap **New item**.

4 Tap the type of file that you want to create.

Note: If you tap **Folder**, Windows 8 creates a new subfolder.

Note: The New Item menu on your system may contain more items than you see here because some programs install their own file types.

An icon for the new file appears in the folder.

5 Type the name that you want to use for the new file.

6 Tap an empty section of the folder.

The name appears under the file's icon.

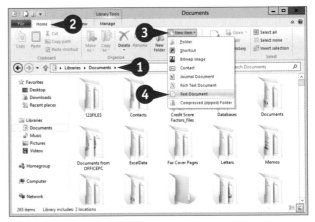

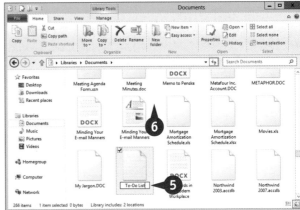

Delete a File

When you have a file that you no longer need, instead of keeping the file to clutter your hard drive, you can delete it.

Make sure that you delete only those documents that you have created yourself or that have been given to you by someone else. Do not delete any of the Windows 8 system files or any files associated with your programs, or your tablet may behave erratically or crash.

Delete a File

1. Open the folder that contains the file that you want to delete.

2. Tap the file that you want to delete.

Note: If you need to remove more than one file, select all the files that you want to delete.

3. Tap the **Home** tab.

4. Tap the top half of the **Delete** button.

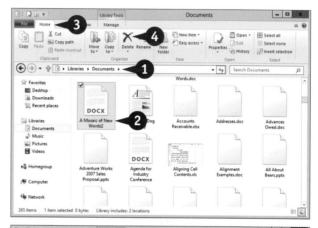

Ⓐ Windows 8 removes the file from the folder.

Note: Another way to delete a file is to tap and drag it to the desktop's Recycle Bin.

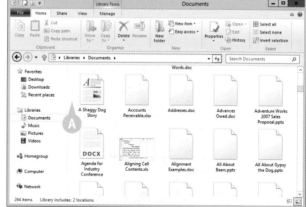

Restore a Deleted File

If you delete a file in error, Windows 8 enables you to restore the file by placing it back in the folder from which you deleted it.

You can restore a deleted file because Windows 8 stores each deleted file in a special folder called the *Recycle Bin,* where the file stays for a few days or a few weeks, depending on how often you empty the bin or how full the folder becomes.

Restore a Deleted File

1 Double-tap the desktop **Recycle Bin**.

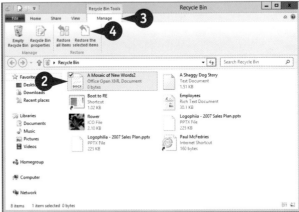

The Recycle Bin folder appears.

2 Tap the file that you want to restore.

3 Tap the **Manage** tab.

4 Tap **Restore the selected items**.

The file disappears from the Recycle Bin and reappears in its original folder.

Zip Up and Extract Compressed Files

An e-mail attachment or a file downloaded from the Internet often arrives in a *compressed* form, which means the file actually contains one or more files that have been compressed to save space. To use the files on your tablet, you need to extract them from the compressed file.

Because a compressed file can contain one or more files, it acts like a kind of folder. Therefore, Windows 8 calls such files *compressed folders, zipped folders,* or *ZIP archives.* You can also create your own compressed folder, which is a good way to send multiple files via e-mail.

Zip Up and Extract Compressed Files

Extract Compressed Files

1 Open the folder containing the compressed folder.

Ⓐ The compressed folder usually appears as a folder icon with a zipper.

2 Tap the compressed folder.

3 Tap the **Extract** tab.

4 Tap **Extract All**.

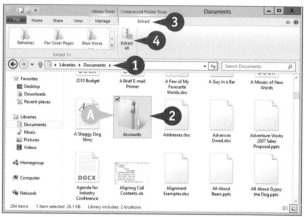

The Select a Destination and Extract Files dialog box of the Extract Wizard appears.

5 Type the location of the folder into which you want the files extracted.

Ⓑ Alternatively, you can tap **Browse** and choose the folder using the Select a Destination dialog box.

6 If you want to open the folder into which you are extracting the files, tap **Show extracted files when complete** (☐ changes to ☑).

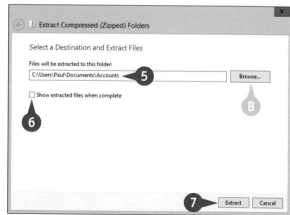

7 Tap **Extract**.

Windows 8 extracts the files.

Zip Up Files to a Compressed Folder

1 Select the files that you want to compress.

2 Tap **Home**.

3 Tap **New item**.

4 Tap **Compressed (zipped) Folder**.

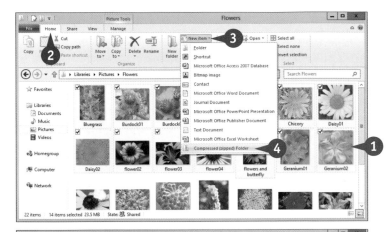

C Windows 8 zips your files into a new compressed folder.

5 Type a name for the compressed folder.

6 Tap an empty section of the folder window.

The name appears under the compressed folder's icon.

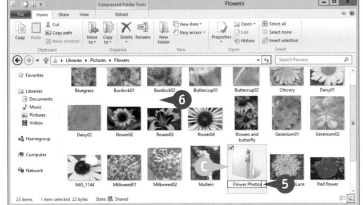

TIPS

Can I extract just a single file from a compressed folder?

Yes. First, double-tap the compressed folder to open it. File Explorer adds a Compressed Folder Tools tab to the ribbon. Select the file that you want to extract, tap **Compressed Folder Tools**, and then use the Extract To gallery to select the destination you want. Alternatively, either tap and drag the file to the desktop or some other location or copy the file to the location that you want.

After I have created a compressed folder, can I add more files to it?

Yes. The easiest way to do this is to tap and drag the file that you want to add and then drop the file in to the compressed folder. If the file and the compressed folder are in separate locations, copy the file, double-tap the compressed folder to open it, and then paste the file.

Add a File to Your SkyDrive

If you are using Windows 8 under a Microsoft account, then as part of that account you get a free online storage area called *SkyDrive*. You can use the SkyDrive app to add any of your files to your SkyDrive. This is useful if you are going to be away from your tablet but still require access to a file. Because the SkyDrive is accessible anywhere you have web access, you can view and work with your file without using your tablet.

Add a File to Your SkyDrive

1 On the Start screen, tap **SkyDrive**.

The SkyDrive app appears.

2 Tap the SkyDrive folder in which you want to store a file.

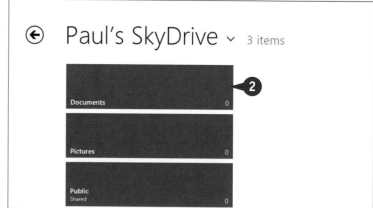

The folder opens.

3 Swipe up from the bottom edge of the screen.

The application bar appears.

4 Tap **Add**.

The Files screen appears.

5 Tap **Files**.

6 Tap the folder that contains the file that you want to upload.

The SkyDrive app displays a list of the files in the selected folder.

7 Tap the file that you want to send to your SkyDrive.

8 Tap **Add to SkyDrive**.

The SkyDrive app uploads the file.

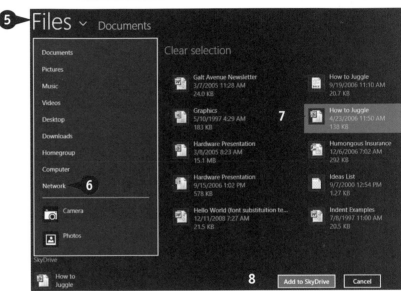

How do I access my SkyDrive online?

The SkyDrive app only uploads existing files. To do more with your SkyDrive, you need to open Internet Explorer and navigate to the SkyDrive site, https://skydrive.live.com. After you are logged in to your SkyDrive, you can use it to create new folders, rename files, delete files, and more.

Can I create new documents using SkyDrive?

Yes. As part of your SkyDrive, Microsoft gives you access to the Office Web Apps, which are scaled-down, online versions of Microsoft Word, Microsoft Excel, Microsoft PowerPoint, and Microsoft OneNote. To create a document using one of these programs, navigate to your online SkyDrive and then tap the Create Word Document button (📄), the Create Excel Workbook button (📄), the Create PowerPoint Presentation button (📄), or the Create OneNote Notebook button (📄).

Share a File with Friends

In these days of ubiquitous social networking, we are immersed in a world of sharing: happenings, links, information, and much more. You can enhance your social contacts and share more of your life with other people by using Windows 8's Share feature to send data.

Windows 8 gets into the spirit of sharing by letting you share app data with other people. For example, you can send a photo, alert a person about a web page, or let someone know about some cool music.

Share a File with Friends

① Using an app, open or select the file that you want to share.

② Swipe left from the right edge of the screen.

The Charms menu appears.

③ Tap **Share**.

The Share pane appears.

4 Tap the app that you want to use to send the selected item.

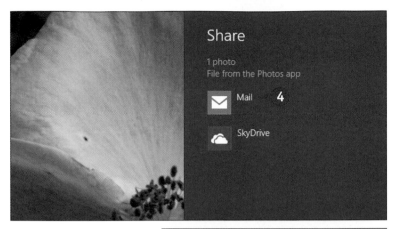

5 Fill in any data that is required to send the item and then initiate the send.

A In Mail, for example, you type the recipient's address, add a subject line, and then tap the Send button (⊞).

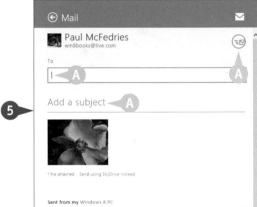

TIP

When I open an app and select an item, why does Windows 8 say, "*App* can't share," in which *App* is the name of the app that I am using?
Windows 8's Share feature is supported only by certain apps. In a default Windows 8 installation, for example, Share works only for items that can be sent via e-mail using the Mail app. However, you may be able to share a wider variety of items by installing third-party apps that extend the Share feature.

CHAPTER 12

Sharing Your Tablet with Others

If you share your tablet with others, this chapter shows you how to create separate user accounts so that each person works only with his own documents, programs, and settings.

PC settings

Personalize

Users

Notifications

Search

Share

General

Privacy

Devices

Wireless

Ease of Access

Sync your settings

HomeGroup

Your account

Paul McFedries
win8books@live.com

You can switch to a local account, but your settings won't sync between the PCs you use.

Switch to a local account

More account settings online

Sign-in options

Change your password

Create a picture password

Create a PIN

Other users

＋ Add a user

Karen
Local Account

Display User Accounts

To work with user accounts, you need to display Windows 8's Users settings.

A *user account* is a collection of Windows 8 folders and settings associated with one person. In this chapter, you learn how to create new user accounts, change a user account's picture, change a user account's password, and delete a user account. To perform any of these tasks, you must first display the Users tab of the PC Settings app.

Display User Accounts

1 Swipe left from the right edge of the screen.

A The Charms menu appears.

2 Tap **Settings**.

The Start settings pane appears.

3 Tap **Change PC settings**.

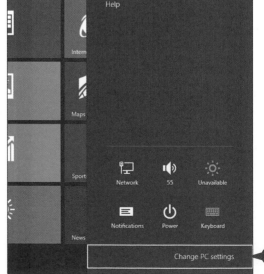

The PC Settings app appears.

④ Tap **Users**.

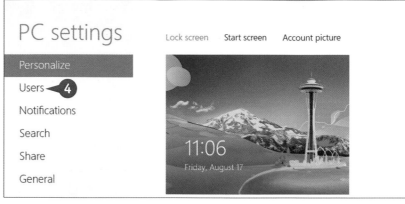

The Users tab appears.

Ⓑ Information about your account appears here. Later, after you have switched to another account, information for that account appears in this spot.

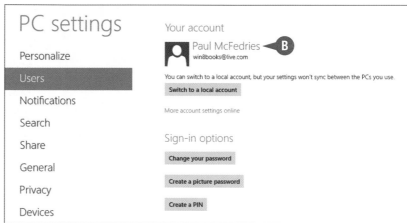

TIP

How do user accounts help me share my tablet with other people?

Without user accounts, anyone who uses your tablet can view and even change your documents, Windows 8 settings, e-mail accounts and messages, Internet Explorer favorites, and more.

With user accounts, users get their own libraries (Documents, Pictures, Music, and so on), personalized Windows 8 settings, e-mail accounts, and favorites. In short, users get their own versions of Windows 8 to personalize without interfering with anyone else's.

Also, user accounts enable you to safely share documents and folders with people who use your tablet and with people on your network.

Create a User Account

If you want to share your tablet with another person, you need to create a user account for that individual. This enables the person to log on to Windows 8 and use the system.

The new user account is completely separate from your own account. This means that the other person can change settings, create documents, and perform other Windows tasks without interfering with your own settings or data. You can create a local user account or a Microsoft account. For maximum privacy, you should safeguard each account with a password.

Create a User Account

1 Display the **Users** tab of the PC Settings app.

Note: See the preceding section, "Display User Accounts," to learn how to display the Users tab.

2 Tap **Add a user**.

The Add a User screen appears.

3 For a local account, tap **Sign in without a Microsoft account**.

Note: If you want to create a Microsoft account instead, follow the steps in the section "Create a Microsoft Account" in Chapter 1.

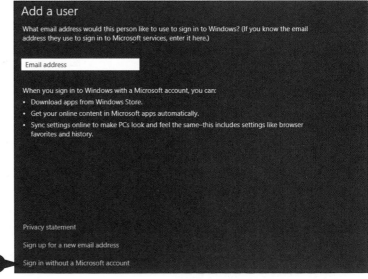

The account options page appears.

4 Tap **Local account**.

The local account version of the password page appears.

5 Type the name that you want to use for the new account.

6 Type the password.

Note: The password characters appear as dots for security reasons.

7 Type the password again.

8 Type a hint that will help you or the user remember the password.

9 Tap **Next**.

The summary page appears.

A If you are setting up an account for a child, you can tap this check box (☐ changes to ☑) to track and control the child's PC usage. See Chapter 13 for details.

10 Tap **Finish**.

Windows 8 creates the account.

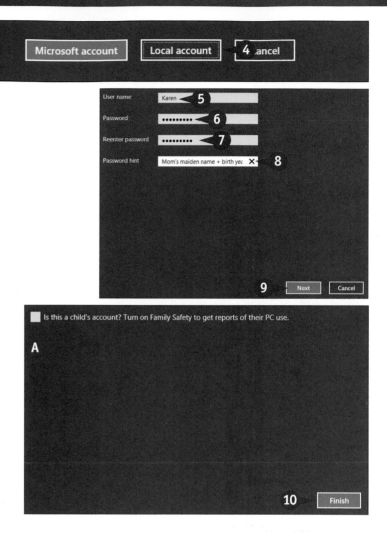

TIP

How do I create a secure password?

It is a good idea to use secure passwords that a nefarious user cannot guess. Here are some guidelines to follow:

• Do not use an obvious password such as the user's account name or the word "password."

• Make sure that the password is at least eight characters long.

• Use at least one character from at least three of the following four sets: lowercase letters, uppercase letters, numbers, and symbols.

Switch between Accounts

After you have created more than one account on your tablet, you can switch between accounts. This is useful when one person is already working in Windows 8 and another person needs to use the tablet.

When you switch to a second account, Windows 8 leaves the original user's programs and windows running. This means that after the second person is finished, the original user can sign on again and continue working as before.

Switch between Accounts

1 On the Start screen, tap your user account tile.

2 Tap the user account to which you want to switch.

Windows 8 prompts you for
the user account password.

③ Type the password.

④ Tap →.

Ⓐ The user's name and picture
now appear on the Start
screen.

TIP

What happens if I forget my password?

When you set up your password as described in the preceding section, "Create a User Account," Windows 8 asks you to supply a hint to help you remember the password. If you cannot remember your password, follow these steps:

① On the sign-on screen, leave the password text box blank.

② Tap →.

Windows 8 tells you that the password is incorrect.

③ Tap **OK** to return to the sign-on screen.

Ⓐ Windows 8 displays the password hint.

Change Your User Account Picture

You can add visual interest to your user account as well as make it a bit easier to tell one user account from another by adding a picture to the account.

When you create a user account, Windows 8 assigns it a default picture, and this picture appears on the user's Start screen tile, the Users tab of the PC Settings app, and the sign-on screen. Unfortunately, this default picture is a generic silhouette of a person's head and upper torso, so it is not very interesting or useful. If you have a more suitable picture, you can change to that instead.

Change Your User Account Picture

1 On the Start screen, tap your user account tile.

2 Tap **Change account picture**.

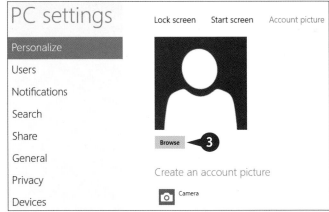

The PC Settings app appears with the Personalize tab displayed.

3 Tap **Browse**.

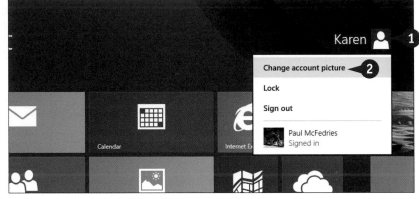

Windows 8 prompts you to choose an account picture.

④ Tap **Files** and then tap the folder that contains the picture that you want to use.

⑤ Tap the picture that you want to use.

⑥ Tap **Choose image**.

④ You are returned to the Personalize tab, which displays the new picture.

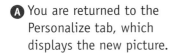

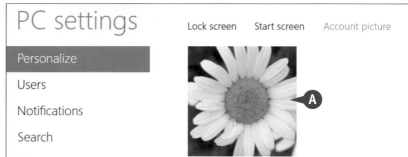

TIP

How do I use a webcam photo as my user account picture?
Follow these steps:

① Follow steps **1** and **2** in this section.

② Tap **Camera**.

The Camera app appears.

③ Position yourself within the screen.

④ Tap the screen to take the picture.

The Camera app displays the photo and adds a rectangle that defines the area of the photo that it will use for your account picture.

⑤ Tap and drag the rectangle to the position that you want.

⑥ Tap and drag the rectangle corners to set the size and shape of the rectangle.

⑦ Tap **OK**.

You are returned to the Personalize tab, which displays the new picture.

Change a User's Password

I f you set up a user account with no password or if you find it difficult to remember your existing password, you can change it.

Assigning a password to each user account is a good practice because, otherwise, someone who picks up the tablet can sign in using an unprotected account. It is also a good practice to assign a strong password to each account so that a malicious user cannot guess it and gain access to the system. You can use Windows 8 to assign a password or create a password that is stronger or easier to remember.

Change a User's Password

1 Sign in to the user account whose password you want to change.

2 Display the **Users** tab of the PC Settings app.

Note: See the section "Display User Accounts," earlier in this chapter, for details.

3 Tap **Change your password**.

Note: If the account has no password, tap **Create a password** instead.

The Change Your Password screen appears.

4 Type your old password.

Note: If the account has no password, you can skip step **4**.

5 Type the new password.

6 Type the new password again.

Ⓐ If you are not sure that you typed the password correctly, tap and hold 👁 to temporarily display the password.

7 Tap **Next**.

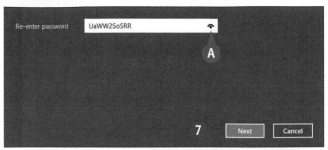

8 Tap **Finish**.

Windows 8 updates the user account password.

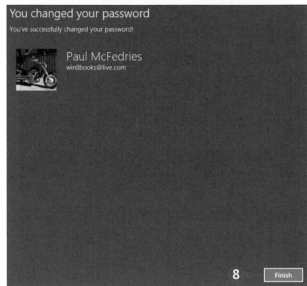

TIP

Are there any other precautions that I can take to protect my password?

Yes, besides creating a strong password as described earlier in this chapter, you should also safeguard your password by following these guidelines:

- Do not tell anyone your password.
- Do not write down your password.
- Make your password easier to remember by using a mnemonic device. For example, you could use the first letters as well as any numbers that appear in the name of a favorite book or movie. For example, from the book *Unbroken: A World War II Story of Survival, Resilience, and Redemption*, you could get the password UaWW2SoSRR.

Delete an Account

If you created a user account temporarily or if you have a user account that is no longer needed or no longer used, you can delete that account.

This reduces the number of users that appear on the Users tab of the PC Settings app, as well as on the Windows 8 sign-on screen, which can make these screens a bit easier to navigate. Deleting a user account also means that Windows 8 reclaims the disk space that the account uses, which gives you more room to store files in your other accounts.

Delete an Account

1 Sign out of the user account that you want to delete.

Note: To sign out of an account, tap the user account tile on the Start screen and then tap **Sign out**.

2 Swipe left from the right edge of the screen and then tap **Search**.

3 Tap **Settings**.

The Settings search pane appears.

4 Type **remove user**.

5 Tap **Remove user accounts**.

The Manage Accounts window appears.

6 Tap the user account that you want to delete.

The Change an Account window appears.

7 Tap **Delete the account**.

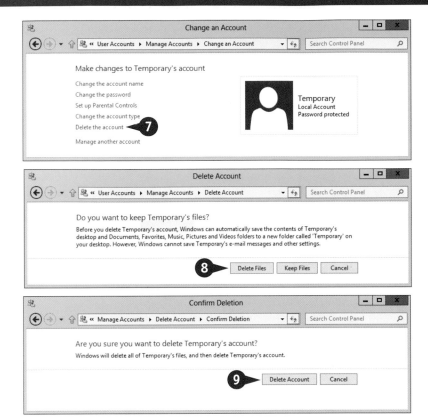

The Delete Account window appears.

8 Tap to specify whether you want to keep or delete the user's personal files.

Note: See the second Tip for information about these two options.

The Confirm Deletion window appears.

9 Tap **Delete Account**.

Windows 8 deletes the account.

TIPS

My user account does not offer the Delete the Account option. Why not?

If yours is the administrator account on the tablet, Windows 8 does not allow you to delete it. Windows 8 requires that a tablet always have at least one administrator account.

What is the difference between the Keep Files and Delete Files options in the Delete Account window?

These options enable you to handle user files two ways:

- Tap **Keep Files** to retain the user's personal files — the contents of his or her Documents folder and desktop. These files are saved on your desktop in a folder named after the user. All other personal items — settings, e-mail accounts and messages, and Internet Explorer favorites — are deleted.

- Tap **Delete Files** to delete all the user's personal files, settings, messages, and favorites.

Create a Homegroup

You can share documents and media easily with other Windows 8 tablets by creating a homegroup on your network. A *homegroup* is a collection of computers that share resources based on a single password. These resources include some or all of the user libraries on each computer and the media devices — such as printers — connected to each computer.

You use one Windows 8 tablet to create the homegroup, and then you use the homegroup password to join your other Windows 8 tablets. See the following section, "Join a Homegroup," for more information.

Create a Homegroup

1 Swipe left from the right edge of the screen and then tap **Settings**.

The Settings pane appears.

2 Tap **Change PC settings**.

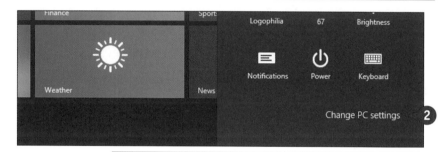

The PC Settings app appears.

3 Tap **HomeGroup**.

4 Tap **Create**.

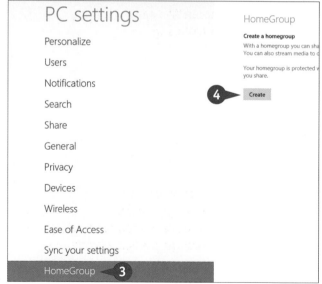

Windows 8 creates the homegroup and displays the Libraries and Devices screen.

5 For each type of file that you want to share with the homegroup, tap the switch to **Shared**.

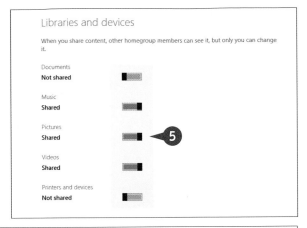

6 If you want devices on your network to be able to play your shared data, tap this switch to **On**.

A Windows 8 displays the homegroup password.

You can now join your other Windows 8 or Windows 7 tablets and computers to the homegroup, as described in the next section.

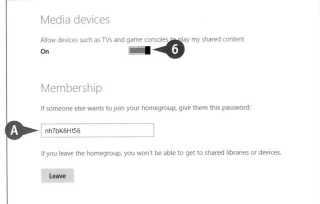

TIPS

I have lost my homegroup password. How do I view it again?
One method is to repeat steps **1** to **3** in this section. Alternatively, swipe left from the right edge of the screen, tap **Search**, and then tap **Settings** to open the Settings search pane. Type **homegroup** and then tap **Change homegroup password**. Tap the **View or print homegroup password** link to see your password.

Is it possible to change the homegroup password?
Yes. Open the Settings search pane, type **homegroup**, and then tap **Change homegroup password**. Tap the **Change the password** link and then tap **Change the password** to generate a new homegroup password. If one or more tablets have already joined the homegroup, you need to provide them with the new password.

Join a Homegroup

If your network has a homegroup, you can join your Windows 8 tablet to that homegroup. This enables you to access shared resources on other homegroup tablets and to share your own resources with the homegroup.

This section assumes that you or someone else on your home network has already set up a homegroup as described in the preceding section, "Create a Homegroup," and that you have the homegroup password.

Join a Homegroup

1 Swipe left from the right edge of the screen and then tap **Settings**.

The Settings pane appears.

2 Tap **Change PC settings**.

The PC Settings app appears.

3 Tap **Homegroup**.

Windows 8 prompts you for the homegroup password.

4 Type the homegroup password.

5 Tap **Join**.

Windows 8 joins the homegroup and displays the Libraries and Devices screen.

6 Tap the switch to **Shared** for each type of file that you want to share with the homegroup.

7 If you want devices on your network to be able to play your shared data, tap this switch to **On**.

You can now access other homegroup tablets and share your files with the homegroup.

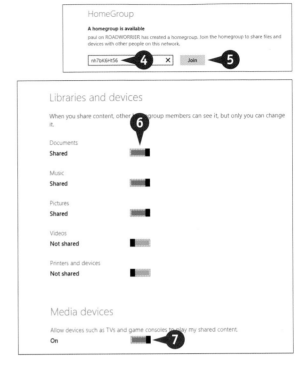

When I try to join a homegroup, Windows 8 tells me my password is not correct. What am I doing wrong?
First, double-check that you have been given the correct homegroup password and that you are typing that password correctly. Second, understand that homegroup passwords are case-sensitive, so you must enter the uppercase and lowercase letters exactly as they appear in the original homegroup settings. Make sure that your touch keyboard does not have Caps Lock turned on.

Can I leave a homegroup if I no longer need it?
Yes. On the Start screen, tap ⊞+❙ to open the Settings pane and then tap **Change PC settings**. Tap **Homegroup** and then tap **Leave**. Windows 8 removes your tablet from the homegroup.

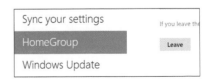

Share a Document or Folder

You can share documents and folders with your homegroup, if your network has one. You can also share a document or folder with other users set up on your tablet.

Sharing a document or folder enables you to work on a file with other people without having to send them a copy of the file. You can set up each document or folder with View or View and Edit permissions. *View permission* means that users cannot make changes to the document or folder; *View and Edit permission* means that users can make changes.

Share a Document or Folder

Share with the Homegroup

1 On the Start screen, tap **Desktop** and then tap 🖥.

File Explorer opens.

2 Open the folder containing the document or subfolder that you want to share.

3 Tap the document or subfolder.

Note: If you want to share more than one item, select all the items.

4 Tap **Share**.

5 Tap **Homegroup (view)**.

A If you want users to make changes to the item, tap **Homegroup (view and edit)** instead.

Share with a Specific User

1 Open the folder containing the document or subfolder that you want to share.

2 Tap the document or subfolder.

3 Tap **Share**.

4 Tap **Specific people**.

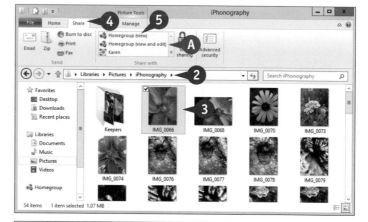

The File Sharing dialog box appears.

5 Tap ☑ and then tap the name of the user.

6 Tap **Add**.

7 Tap ☑ and then tap the permission level.

Note: Read permission is the same as View, and Read/Write is the same as View and Edit.

8 Tap **Share**.

Windows 8 shares the document or folder.

Ⓑ Be sure to give the user the address that appears here.

9 Tap **Done**.

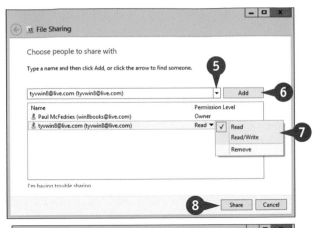

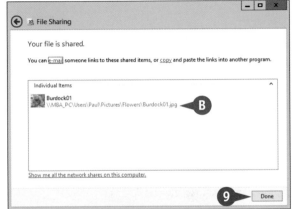

TIPS

How do the other users access the shared document or folder?

You need to send them the address that appears in the final File Sharing window. You have two choices: Tap **e-mail** to send the address via e-mail or tap **copy** to copy the address to memory. You can then open a program such as WordPad, tap **Edit**, and then tap **Paste** to paste the address.

Can I see all the documents and folders that I am sharing with other users?

Yes, you can do this in two ways. In the final File Sharing window, tap **Show me all the network shares on this computer**. Alternatively, in any folder window, tap **Network** and then double-tap your tablet.

CHAPTER 13

Implementing Security

Threats to your computing-related security and privacy often come from the Internet and from someone simply using your tablet while you are not around. To protect yourself and your family, you need to understand these threats and know what you can do to thwart them.

Understanding Windows 8 Security

Before you get to the details of securing your tablet, it helps to take a step back and look at the security and privacy tools that Windows 8 makes available.

These tools include your Windows 8 user account password, User Account Control, Family Safety, Windows Firewall, Windows Defender, Internet Explorer's antiphishing features, and Windows Live Mail's antispam features. Taken all together, these features represent a *defense-in-depth* security strategy that uses multiple layers to keep you and your data safe and private.

User Account Password

Windows 8 security begins with assigning a password to each user account on the tablet. This prevents unauthorized users from accessing the system, and it enables you to lock your tablet. See the section "Lock Your Tablet," later in this chapter.

User Account Control

User Account Control asks you to confirm certain actions that could conceivably harm your system. When you are using your main Windows 8 user account, which is your tablet's administrative account, you tap **Yes** to continue; for all other accounts, you must enter the administrative account's password to continue.

Family Safety

If one or more children use your tablet, you can use Windows 8's Family Safety feature to protect them from inadvertently running certain programs, playing unsuitable games, and using the tablet at inappropriate times. See the section "Set Up Family Safety," later in this chapter.

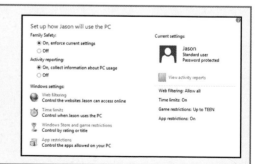

Windows Firewall

Because when your tablet is connected to the Internet, it is possible for another person to access your tablet and infect it with a virus or cause other damage, Windows 8 comes with its Windows Firewall feature turned on. This prevents intruders from accessing your tablet while you are online.

Windows Defender

Spyware is a software program that installs itself on your tablet without your knowledge or consent. This type of program surreptitiously gathers data from your tablet, steals your passwords, displays advertisements, and hijacks your web browser. To prevent spyware from installing on your tablet, Windows 8 includes the Windows Defender program.

Malware Detected
Windows Defender is taking action to clean detected malware

InPrivate Web Browsing

The Internet Explorer web browser normally collects data as you navigate from site to site. Most of this data is used to improve your browsing experience, but it can also be used to track your online activities. If you plan on visiting private or sensitive sites, you can turn on InPrivate Browsing, which tells Internet Explorer not to collect any data during your browsing session. See the section "Browse the Web Privately," later in this chapter.

Reset Your PC

Your tablet contains lots of information about you, including your personal files, your Internet Explorer pinned sites, your e-mail messages, and your Windows 8 settings. If you plan on selling or donating your tablet, you do not want the recipient to see this data. To prevent that, you can use the Reset Your PC feature to securely remove your data while installing a fresh copy of Windows 8. See the section "Reset Your Tablet to Preserve Privacy," later in this chapter.

Remove everything and reinstall Windows
If you want to recycle your PC or start over completely, you can reset it to its factory settings.
Get started

Check the Action Center for Security Problems

In Windows 8, the Action Center displays messages about the current state of your tablet. In particular, the Action Center warns you if your tablet has any current security problems.

For example, the Action Center tells you if your tablet does not have virus protection installed or if the Windows Defender spyware database is out of date. The Action Center will also warn you if your tablet is not set up to download updates automatically and if important security features such as User Account Control are turned off.

Check the Action Center for Security Problems

1 Swipe left from the right edge, tap **Search**, and then tap **Settings**.

The Settings search pane appears.

2 Type **action**.

Windows 8 displays the "action" search results.

3 Tap **Action Center**.

The Action Center window appears.

4 Review the messages in the **Security** section.

5 Tap a message button to resolve the security issue, such as tapping **Turn on now** if Windows Defender is turned off.

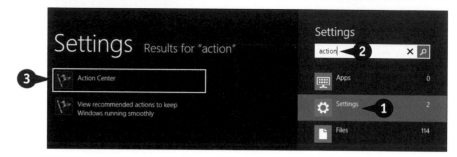

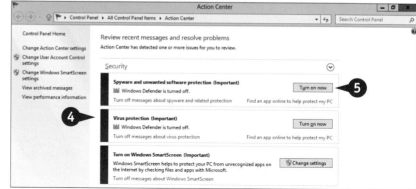

6 Tap **Security**.

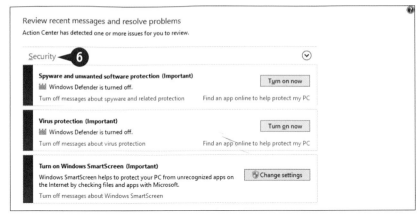

7 Scroll down the Action Center window.

Ⓐ The Action Center displays a summary of all your system's security settings.

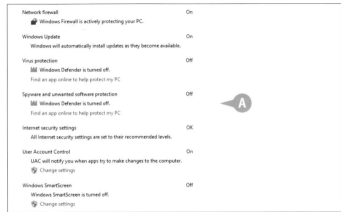

TIP

Is there a quicker way to see the Action Center messages?

Yes, if you are working in the Desktop app, you can view the Action Center messages and open the Action Center more quickly by following these steps:

1 Tap the **Action Center** icon (▣) in the taskbar's notification area.

Ⓐ The current Action Center messages appear here.

2 To launch the Action Center, tap **Open Action Center**.

The Action Center appears.

279

Create a Picture Password

You can make it much easier to sign in to your Windows 8 tablet by creating a picture password.

If you find that it is taking you an inordinate amount of time to sign in to Windows 8 using your tablet's touch keyboard, you can switch to a picture password instead. In this case, your "password" is a series of three gestures — any combination of a tap, a straight line, or a circle — that you apply to a photo. Windows 8 displays the photo at startup, and you repeat your gestures, in order, to sign in to Windows.

Create a Picture Password

1 Swipe left from the right edge, tap **Search**, and then tap **Settings**.

The Settings search pane appears.

2 Type **password**.

Windows 8 displays the "password" search results.

3 Tap **Create or change picture password**.

The PC Settings app appears and displays the Users tab.

4 Tap **Create a picture password**.

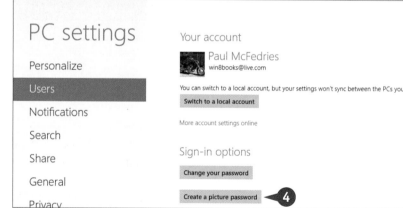

Windows 8 prompts you for your account password.

5 Type your password.

6 Tap **OK**.

The Welcome to Picture Password screen appears.

7 Tap **Choose picture**.

Is a picture password safe to use?

Most of the time. The biggest drawback to using a picture password is that it is possible for a malicious user to view and possibly even record your gestures using a camera. Unlike a regular text password for which the characters appear as dots to prevent someone from seeing them, your gestures have no such protection.

Does the picture password replace my existing text password?

No, your picture password is applied to your user account along with your existing text-based password. That is, the picture password does *not* replace your text password. As you see in the next Tips section, it is not difficult to bypass the picture password and sign in using the text password, so it is vital that you still protect your tablet with a strong text password.

continued ▶

In the same way that you should not choose a regular account password that is extremely obvious, such as the word *password* or your username, you should take care to avoid creating an obvious picture password. For example, if you are using a photo showing three faces, an obvious picture password would be a tap on each face. A good picture password not only uses all three available gestures, but also uses them in nonobvious ways.

To ensure that you have memorized your picture password, you should sign out of your account a few times and then sign back on using the picture password.

Create a Picture Password (continued)

The Files screen appears.

8 Tap the picture that you want to use.

9 Tap **Open**.

The How's This Look? screen appears.

10 Drag the picture so that the image is positioned where you prefer.

11 Tap **Use this picture**.

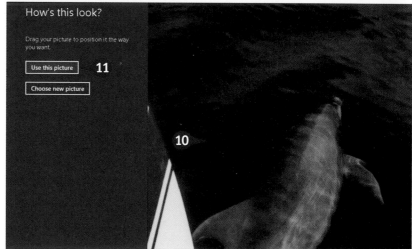

The Set Up Your Gestures screen appears.

12 Use your finger or a stylus to draw three gestures.

13 Repeat the gestures to confirm.

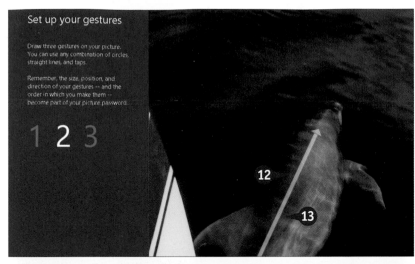

14 Tap **Finish**.

The next time that you sign in to Windows 8, you will be prompted to enter your picture password gestures.

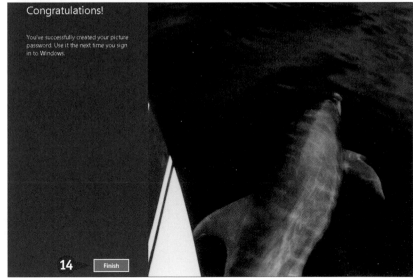

TIPS

What happens if I forget my gestures?

If you forget the gestures in your picture password, tap **Switch to password** on the sign-on screen to sign in with your regular password. To get a reminder of your picture password gestures, follow steps **1** to **3** in this section, tap **Change picture password**, type your user account password, and tap **OK**. In the Change Your Picture Password screen, tap **Replay**. Tap the picture to see each gesture.

Can I change my picture password?

If you feel that your picture password has been compromised — for example, someone witnessed your sign-on, if you want to change your gestures, or if you have grown tired of the original picture that you chose, you can change your picture password. Open the Change Picture Password screen as described in the preceding tip, choose a new picture, if necessary, and then run through your gestures.

Lock Your Tablet

You can enhance your tablet's security by locking the device when you leave it unattended.

Protecting your account with a password prevents someone from logging on to your account, but what happens when you leave your tablet unattended? If you remain logged on to the system, any person who picks up your tablet can use it to view and change files. To prevent this, lock your tablet. After your tablet is locked, anyone who tries to use your tablet will first have to enter your password.

Lock Your Tablet

Lock Your Tablet

1 On the Start screen, tap your user account tile.

2 Tap **Lock**.

Windows 8 locks your tablet and displays the Lock screen.

Unlock Your Tablet

1 On the Lock screen, swipe up to display the sign-on screen.

A The word "Locked" appears under your username.

2 Tap inside the **Password** text box.

3 Type your password.

4 Tap →.

Windows 8 unlocks your tablet and restores your desktop.

TIP

I use the Lock command frequently. Is there a way to make it easier to access?

Yes, there are two faster methods that you can use. The first method is to display the standard touch keyboard and tap ⊞+🔒. The second method is to configure Windows 8 to automatically lock the tablet after it has been idle for a specified amount of time:

1 Swipe in from the right edge, tap **Search**, and then tap **Settings** to open the Settings search pane.

2 Type **lock tablet**.

3 Tap **Lock the tablet when I leave it alone for a period of time**.

4 Tap **On resume, display logon screen** (☐ changes to ☑).

5 Use the **Wait** text box to set the number of minutes of idle time after which Windows 8 locks your tablet.

6 Tap **OK**.

Set Up Family Safety

If your children have tablet access, you can protect them from malicious content by setting up parental controls, called the *Family Safety* feature, for activities such as web surfing, playing games, and running programs. Family Safety enables you to set specific limits on how your children perform various activities on the tablet. For example, the Windows Web Filter lets you specify allowable websites, restrict sites based on content, and block file downloads.

Before you can apply the Family Safety controls, you must set up a Windows 8 user account for each child. See the section "Create a User Account" in Chapter 12.

Set Up Family Safety

Activate Family Safety

1 Swipe left from the right edge, tap **Search**, and then tap **Settings**.

The Settings search pane appears.

2 Type **family**.

Windows 8 displays the "family" search results.

3 Tap **Family Safety**.

The Family Safety window appears.

4 Tap the user that you want to work with.

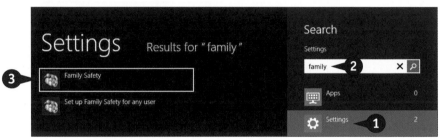

The User Settings window appears.

5 Tap **On, enforce current settings** (○ changes to ◉).

Windows 8 turns on parental controls for the user.

Set Web Restrictions

6 Tap **Web Filtering**.

The Web Filtering window appears.

7 Tap *User* **can only use the websites I allow** (○ changes to ◉).

8 If you want to control specific sites, tap **Allow or block specific websites**, type the site address, and then tap **Allow** or **Block**.

9 Tap **Web Restrictions** and then tap a web-restriction level (○ changes to ◉).

10 Tap **User Settings**.

The web restrictions are set, and you are returned to the User Settings window.

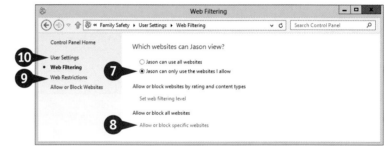

TIPS

How do I prevent my kids from downloading files?

Blocking downloads is a good idea because it reduces the risk of infecting the tablet with viruses or other malicious software. In the User Settings window, tap **Web Filtering** and then tap **Web Restrictions** to display the Web Restrictions window. Swipe down to the bottom of the window and tap **Block file downloads** (☐ changes to ☑). Tap **User Settings**.

Can I choose which game rating system Windows 8 uses?

Yes, Windows 8 supports several game rating systems, including classifications from the Entertainment Software Rating Board (the default system), Computer Entertainment Rating Organization, and Game Rating Board. Return to the Family Safety window, tap **Rating Systems**, tap the system that you want to use (○ changes to ◉), and then tap **Accounts to Monitor**.

continued ▶ **287**

After you have parental controls activated, you can set up specific restrictions. For example, you can allow and block specific websites, and you can set the web-restriction level to determine the types of sites your children can access.

You can also set up times when children are not allowed to use the tablet. Windows 8's Family Safety feature also enables you to set the maximum game rating that kids can play, allow or block specific games, and allow or block specific programs.

Set Up Family Safety (continued)

Set Tablet Time Limits

11 Tap **Time limits**.

The Time Limits window appears.

12 Tap **Curfew**.

13 Tap *User* **can only use the PC during the time ranges I allow** (○ changes to ⦿).

14 Tap each hour that you want to block access to the tablet.

Ⓐ Blocked hours appear in blue.

Ⓑ Allowed hours appear in white.

15 Tap **User Settings**.

The time limits are set, and you are returned to the User Settings window.

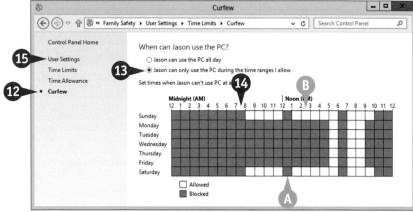

Restrict Game Usage

16 Tap **Windows Store and game restrictions**.

The Game and Windows Store Restrictions window appears.

17 Tap *User* **can only use games and Windows Store apps I allow** (○ changes to ◉).

18 Tap **Rating Level**.

The Rating Level window appears.

19 Tap the maximum rating that you want the user to play (○ changes to ◉).

20 Tap **User Settings**.

The game restrictions are set.

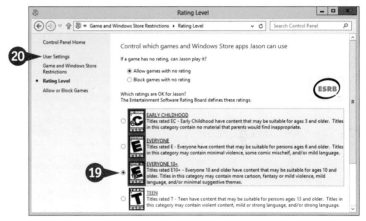

TIPS

Can I block a specific game?
Yes. In the Game and Windows Store Restrictions window, tap **Allow or block specific games** to display the Allow or Block Games window, which shows all the games installed on your tablet. For the game that you want to block, tap the **Always Block** option (○ changes to ◉) and then tap **User Settings**.

Can I prevent my kids from running certain programs?
Yes. In the User Settings window, tap **App restrictions** to display the App Restrictions window. Tap *User* **can only use the apps I allow**, where *User* is the name of the user. In the list, tap the check box for each program that you want the user to be able to run (☐ changes to ☑). Tap **User Settings**.

Browse the Web Privately

If you visit sensitive or private websites, you can tell Internet Explorer not to save any browsing history for those sites.

If you regularly visit private websites or websites that contain sensitive or secret data, you can ensure that no one else sees any data for such sites by deleting your browsing history, as described in the Tip. However, if you visit such sites only occasionally, deleting your entire browsing history is overkill. A better solution is to turn on Internet Explorer's InPrivate Browsing feature before you visit private sites. This tells Internet Explorer to temporarily stop saving any browsing history.

Browse the Web Privately

1 On the Start screen, tap **Internet Explorer**.

2 Swipe down from the top edge of the screen.

Internet Explorer displays the tab bar.

3 Tap the More button (⊙).

4 Tap **New InPrivate tab**.

A new Internet Explorer tab appears.

🅐 The InPrivate indicator appears in the address bar.

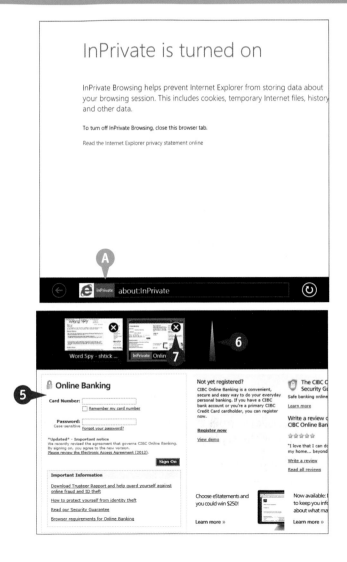

🅐

InPrivate about:InPrivate

5 Surf to and interact with websites as you normally would.

6 When you are done, swipe down from the top edge of the screen.

7 Tap ⊗ on the InPrivate Browsing tab.

Internet Explorer closes the InPrivate Browsing tab and turns off InPrivate Browsing.

What is the browsing history?

Internet Explorer maintains a list of the sites that you visit, as well as copies of page text, images, and other content so that sites load faster the next time you view them. Internet Explorer also saves text and passwords that you have typed into forms, the names of files that you have downloaded, and *cookies*, which are small text files that store information such as site preferences and site logon data.

Saving this history is dangerous because other people who use your computer can just as easily visit or view information about those sites. You eliminate this risk by visiting such sites using a private browsing session.

If you want to delete your browsing history, swipe left from the right edge, tap **Settings**, tap **Internet Options**, and then tap **Delete**.

Clear Your Private Information

One of the benefits of the Windows 8 Start screen is that it uses *live tiles* that display constantly updated information. This includes newly received e-mail and instant messages, the current music you are playing, the photo slide show you are playing, and the latest information from the Weather and Finance apps. However, this can be a privacy problem because anyone walking by your tablet can see this information with a quick glance. To prevent this, you can temporarily clear all your private information from the Start screen tiles.

Clear Your Private Information

1 Swipe left from the right edge of the screen.

The Charms menu appears.

2 Tap **Settings**.

The Settings pane appears.

3 Tap **Tiles**.

The Tiles Settings pane appears.

④ Tap **Clear**.

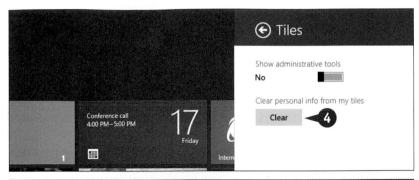

Windows 8 removes all your personal information from the Start screen.

TIPS

Can I prevent an app from ever showing private information in its tile?

Yes, you can turn off the updating permanently for the tile. Swipe down on the tile and then tap **Turn live tile off**.

Can I prevent an app from displaying private information in a notification?

Some apps present a notification when new information comes in to your tablet. For example, the Messaging app lets you know when a new instant message has arrived. Because some of these notifications can contain private information, you might want to turn off the notifications for certain apps. Follow steps **1** and **2** in this section to display the Settings pane and tap **Change PC settings** to open the PC Settings app. Tap **Notifications** and then beside each app for which you want notifications disabled, tap the switch to **Off**.

Reset Your Tablet to Preserve Privacy

As you use your tablet, you accumulate a large amount of personal data: documents, installed apps, Internet Explorer favorites, e-mail messages, photos, and much more. If you are selling your tablet or giving it away, you probably do not want the recipient to have access to all that personal data. To prevent this, you can reset the tablet, which deletes all your personal data and reinstalls a fresh copy of Windows 8.

Reset Your Tablet to Preserve Privacy

Note: This section assumes that you have copied your personal files to a backup destination, such as an external hard drive.

1. Insert your Windows 8 installation media.

2. Swipe from the right edge to open the Charms menu and then tap **Settings**.

   The Settings pane appears.

3. Tap **Change PC settings**.

   The PC Settings app opens.

4. Tap **General**.

5. Under **Remove everything and reinstall Windows**, tap **Get started**.

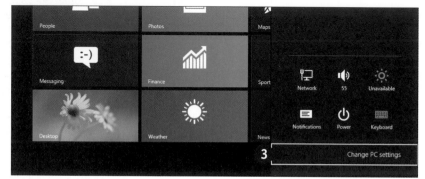

Windows 8 displays an overview of the reset process.

6 Tap **Next**.

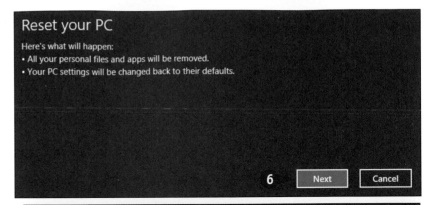

Windows 8 asks how you want to remove your personal files.

7 Tap the removal option that you want.

Note: For more information about the removal options, see the first Tip.

The Ready to Reset Your PC screen appears.

8 Tap **Reset**.

Windows 8 resets your tablet.

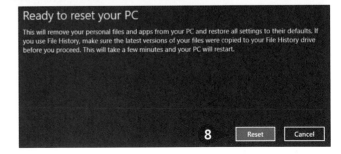

TIPS

What is the difference between removing my files thoroughly or quickly?

The Just Remove My Files option deletes your data in the sense that after Windows is reset, it can no longer work with or see the data. However, the data remains on the tablet's hard drive, so a person with special tools can access the data. The Fully Clean the Drive option prevents this by overwriting your information with random data, which can take quite a bit of time but is much more secure.

Can I still reset my tablet if I do not have my Windows 8 installation media?

Yes, you can use a Windows 8 recovery drive instead. This is a USB flash drive that contains the Windows 8 recovery tools. To learn how to create such a drive, see the section "Create a Recovery Drive" in Chapter 14.

Maintaining Windows 8

To keep your tablet running smoothly, maintain top performance, and reduce the risk of problems, you need to perform some routine maintenance chores. This chapter shows you how to delete unnecessary files, create a recovery drive, back up your files, and more.

Check Hard Drive Free Space

To ensure that your tablet's hard disk does not become full, you should periodically check how much free space it has left. This is important because if you run out of room on your hard drive, you cannot install more programs or create more documents, and your tablet's performance will suffer.

Of particular concern is the hard drive on which Windows 8 is installed, usually drive C. If this hard drive's free space gets low — say, less than about 5GB — Windows 8 runs slowly.

Check Hard Drive Free Space

Note: You can also check the free space on a memory card or flash drive. Before you continue, insert the card or drive.

1 Swipe left from the right edge to display the Charms menu and then tap **Search**.

2 Type **computer**.

Windows 8 displays the "computer" search results.

3 Tap **Computer**.

The Computer window appears.

4 Tap the **View** tab.

5 Tap **Tiles**.

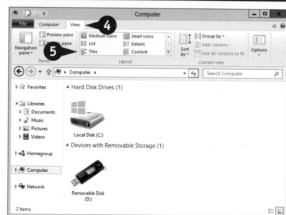

Information about each drive appears along with the drive icon.

Ⓐ This value tells you the amount of free space on the drive.

Ⓑ This value tells you the total amount of space on the drive.

Ⓒ This bar gives you a visual indication of how much disk space the drive is using.

Ⓓ Windows is installed on the drive with the Windows logo (🪟).

Ⓔ The used portion of the bar appears blue when a drive still has sufficient disk space.

Ⓕ The used portion of the bar turns red when a drive's disk space becomes low.

⑥ Tap ▣ to close the Computer window.

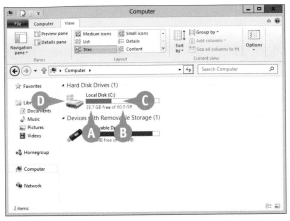

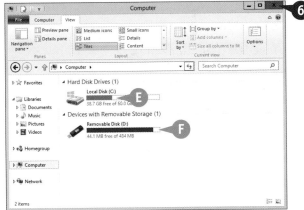

How often should I check my hard drive free space?

With normal tablet use, you should check your hard drive free space about once a month. If you install programs, create large files, or download media frequently, you should probably check your free space every couple of weeks.

What can I do if my hard drive space is getting low?

You can do three things:

- **Delete documents:** If you have documents — particularly media files such as images, music, and videos — that you are sure that you no longer need, delete them.

- **Remove programs:** If you have programs that you no longer use, uninstall them; see Chapter 2, "Working with Apps," for more information.

- **Run Disk Cleanup:** Use the Disk Cleanup program to delete files that Windows 8 no longer uses. See the next section, "Delete Unnecessary Files."

Delete Unnecessary Files

To free up hard drive space on your tablet and keep Windows 8 running efficiently, you can use the Disk Cleanup program to delete files that your system no longer needs.

Although today's hard drives are quite sizeable, it is still possible to run low on disk space, particularly because today's applications and media files are larger than ever. Run Disk Cleanup any time that your hard drive free space gets too low. If hard drive space is not a problem, run Disk Cleanup every two or three months.

Delete Unnecessary Files

1 Swipe left from the right edge of the screen, tap **Search**, and then tap **Settings**.

The Settings search pane appears.

2 Type **disk cleanup**.

Windows 8 displays the "disk cleanup" search results.

3 Tap **Free up disk space by deleting unnecessary files**.

If your tablet has more than one drive, the Drive Selection dialog box appears.

4 Tap the **Drives** ⊡ and then tap the hard drive that you want to clean up.

5 Tap **OK**.

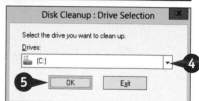

After a few moments, the Disk Cleanup dialog box appears.

Ⓐ This area displays the total amount of drive space that you can free up.

Ⓑ This area displays the amount of drive space the activated options will free up.

6 Tap the check box (☐ changes to ☑) for each file type that you want to delete.

Ⓒ This area displays a description of the highlighted file type.

7 Tap **OK**.

Disk Cleanup asks you to confirm that you want to delete the file types.

8 Tap **Delete Files**.

The unnecessary files are deleted.

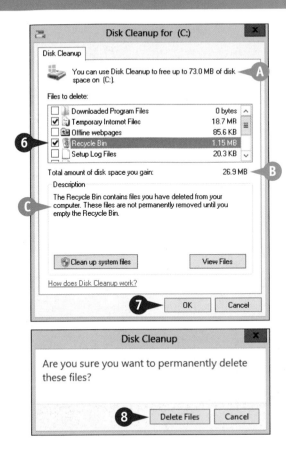

TIP

What types of files does Disk Cleanup delete?
The file types that it can delete include the following:

- **Downloaded program files:** Small web page programs downloaded onto your hard drive.
- **Temporary Internet files:** Web page copies stored on your hard drive for faster viewing.
- **Offline web pages:** Web page copies stored on your hard drive for offline viewing.
- **Recycle Bin:** Files that you have deleted since you last emptied your Recycle Bin.
- **Temporary files:** Files used by programs to store temporary data.
- **Thumbnails:** Miniature versions of images and other content used in folder windows.

Check Your Hard Drive for Errors

To keep your system running smoothly, you should periodically check your hard drive for errors and fix any errors that come up.

Because hard drive errors such as bad sectors can cause files to become corrupted, which may prevent you from running a program or opening a document, you can use the Check Disk program to look for and fix hard drive errors.

Check Your Hard Drive for Errors

1 On the Start screen, tap **Desktop** and then tap the File Explorer button (▦).

File Explorer opens.

2 Tap **Computer**.

3 Tap the hard drive that you want to check.

4 Tap the **Computer** tab.

5 Tap **Properties**.

The hard drive's Properties dialog box appears.

6 Tap the **Tools** tab.

7 Tap **Check**.

Ⓐ If Windows 8 tells you that the drive has no errors, you can tap **Cancel** and skip the rest of these steps.

❽ Otherwise, tap **Scan drive**.

Windows 8 checks the hard drive.

❾ When the check is complete, tap **Close**.

Note: If Check Disk finds any errors, follow the instructions provided by the program.

TIPS

What is a "bad sector"?
A *sector* is a small storage location on your hard drive. When Windows 8 saves a file on the drive, it divides the file into pieces and stores each piece in a separate sector. A bad sector is one that, through physical damage or some other cause, can no longer be used to reliably store data.

How often should I check for hard drive errors?
If you use your tablet daily, you should perform the hard drive check about once a week. If you use your tablet only occasionally, you can perform the hard drive check about once a month. Remember, too, that if you have an external hard drive attached to your tablet, it is a good idea to check that drive for errors as well, perhaps every two weeks or so.

Refresh Your Tablet

If you find that your tablet is running slowly or that frequent program glitches are hurting your productivity, you can often solve these problems by resetting your tablet's system files.

The Refresh Your PC feature reinstalls a fresh copy of Windows 8. It also saves the documents, images, and other files in your user account, some of your settings, and any Windows 8 apps that you have installed. However, Refresh Your PC does *not* save any other system settings — which are reverted to their defaults — or any desktop programs that you installed, if your tablet supports that feature.

Refresh Your Tablet

1. Swipe left from the right edge of the screen.

2. Tap **Search**.

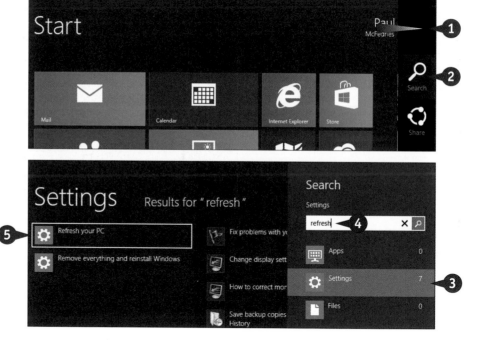

The Search pane appears.

3. Tap **Settings**.

The Settings search pane appears.

4. Type **refresh**.

Windows 8 displays the "refresh" search results.

5. Tap **Refresh your PC**.

A bulleted list appears, outlining the process.

6 Insert your Windows 8 installation media or a Windows 8 recovery drive.

Note: See the following section, "Create a Recovery Drive," to learn how to create a USB recovery drive.

7 Tap **Next**.

8 Tap **Refresh**.

Your system files are refreshed, and your tablet restarts.

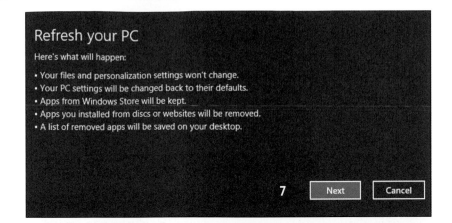

TIP

How do I refresh my tablet if I cannot start Windows?

If system problems are preventing Windows 8 from starting, you can also run Refresh Your PC from your Windows installation media:

1 Insert the media and then restart your tablet.

2 Boot to the media.

Note: How you boot to the media depends on your system.

The Windows Setup dialog box appears.

3 Tap **Next**.

4 Tap **Repair your computer**.

5 Tap **Troubleshoot**.

6 Tap **Refresh Your PC**.

7 Tap **Next**.

8 Tap **Windows 8**.

9 Tap **Refresh**.

Create a Recovery Drive

You can make it easier to troubleshoot and recover from tablet problems by creating a USB recovery drive.

If a problem prevents you from booting your tablet, you must boot using some other drive. If you have your Windows 8 installation media, you can boot using that drive. If you do not have the installation media, you can still recover if you have created a recovery drive. This is a USB flash drive that contains the Windows 8 recovery environment, which enables you to refresh or reset your PC, recover a system image, and more.

Create a Recovery Drive

1 Insert the USB flash drive that you want to use.

2 Swipe left from the right edge of the screen, tap **Search**, and then tap **Settings**.

The Settings search pane appears.

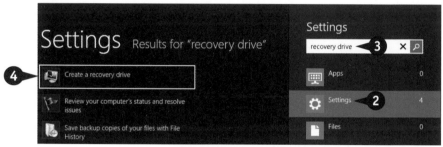

3 Type **recovery drive**.

Windows 8 displays the "recovery drive" search results.

4 Tap **Create a recovery drive**.

The User Account Control dialog box appears.

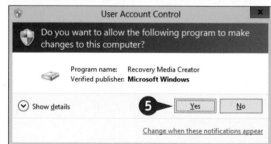

5 Tap **Yes**.

Note: If you are using a standard account, enter your PC's administrator credentials to continue.

The Recovery Drive wizard appears.

6 Tap **Next**.

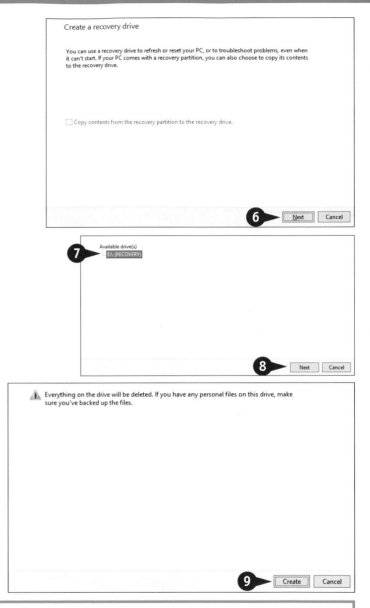

Create a recovery drive

You can use a recovery drive to refresh or reset your PC, or to troubleshoot problems, even when it can't start. If your PC comes with a recovery partition, you can also choose to copy its contents to the recovery drive.

☐ Copy contents from the recovery partition to the recovery drive.

6 → Next   Cancel

The Recovery Drive wizard prompts you to choose the USB flash drive.

7 Tap the drive, if it is not selected already.

8 Tap **Next**.

Available drive(s)
7 → E:\ (RECOVERY)

8 → Next   Cancel

The Recovery Drive wizard warns you that all the data on the drive will be deleted.

9 Tap **Create**.

The wizard formats the drive and copies the recovery tools and data to it.

10 Tap **Finish**.

⚠ Everything on the drive will be deleted. If you have any personal files on this drive, make sure you've backed up the files.

9 → Create   Cancel

TIPS

Can I use any USB flash drive as a recovery drive?
No. To use a USB flash drive as a recovery drive, the drive must have a capacity of at least 256MB. Also, Windows 8 will erase all data on the drive, so make sure that the flash drive does not contain any files you want to keep. If it does, be sure to move those files to a different drive before you begin this procedure.

How can I make sure that the recovery drive works properly?
To make sure that your recovery drive works properly, you should test it by booting your tablet to the drive. Insert the recovery drive and then restart your tablet. How you boot to the drive depends on your system. For example, some tablets display a menu of boot devices, and you select the USB drive from that menu.

Keep a Backup History of Your Files

You can make it easier to recover earlier versions of your files by saving copies of your files to an external drive.

Sometimes it is not good enough to back up a file by making a copy. For example, if you make frequent changes to a file, you might want to copy not only the current version, but also the versions from a hour ago, a day ago, and so on. These previous versions of a file are called its *file history,* and you can save this data for all your documents by activating the File History feature.

Keep a Backup History of Your Files

Set the File History Drive

1 Connect an external drive to your PC.

Note: The drive should have enough capacity to hold your files, so an external hard drive is probably best.

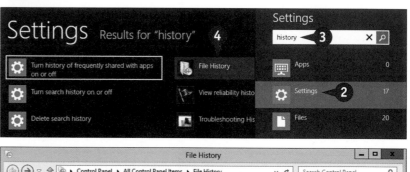

2 Swipe left from the right edge of the screen, tap **Search**, and then tap **Settings**.

The Settings search pane appears.

3 Type **history**.

Windows 8 displays the "history" search results.

4 Tap **File History**.

The File History window appears.

Ⓐ If Windows 8 detects an external hard drive, it displays the drive here.

If this is the correct drive, you can skip steps **5** to **7**.

5 Tap **Select drive**.

The Select Drive control panel appears.

6 Tap the drive that you want to use.

7 Tap **OK**.

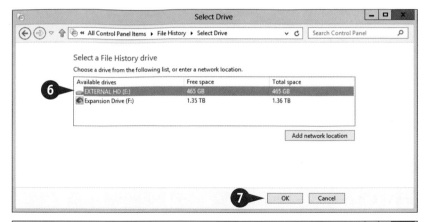

Activate File History

1 Tap **Turn on**.

Windows 8 activates File History and begins saving copies of your files to the external drive.

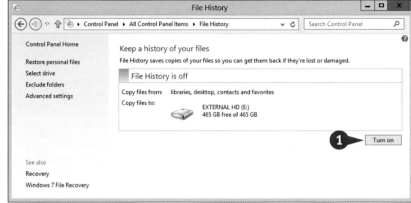

TIPS

What can I do if I do not have an external hard drive?

If you do not have an external drive or if your drives do not have enough capacity, you can use a network folder to store your file history. In the File History window, tap **Change drive** and then tap **Add network location**. In the Select Folder dialog box, open a computer or tablet on your network, select a shared folder to which you have permission to add files, and then tap **Select Folder**.

Is it okay to disconnect the external hard drive temporarily?

If you need to remove the external drive temporarily — for example, if you need to use the port for another device — you should turn off File History before disconnecting the external drive. Follow steps **1** to **4** in this section to open the File History window and then tap **Turn off**.

Restore a File from Your History

I
f you improperly edit, accidentally delete, or corrupt a file through a system crash, you can restore a previous version of the file.

Why would you want to revert to a previous version of a file? One reason is that you might have improperly edited the file by deleting or changing important data. You may be able to retrieve that data from an earlier version. Another reason is that the file might become corrupted if the program crashes. You can get a working version of the file back by restoring a previous version.

Restore a File from Your History

1 Swipe left from the right edge of the screen, tap **Search**, and then tap **Settings**.

The Settings search pane appears.

2 Type **history**.

Windows 8 displays the "history" search results.

3 Tap **File History**.

The File History window appears.

4 Tap **Restore personal files**.

The Home - File History window appears.

5 Double-tap the library that contains the file you want to restore.

The library opens.

6 Open the folder that contains the file.

7 Tap the Previous Version button (⏮) until you open the version of the folder that you want to use.

8 Tap the file that you want to restore.

9 Tap the Restore to Original Location button (↻).

If the original folder has a file with the same name, File History asks what you want to do.

10 Select an option:

• Tap **Replace the file in the destination folder** to overwrite the existing file with the previous version.

• Tap **Skip this file** to do nothing.

• Tap **Choose the file to keep in the destination folder** to decide which file you prefer to keep.

Windows 8 restores the previous version.

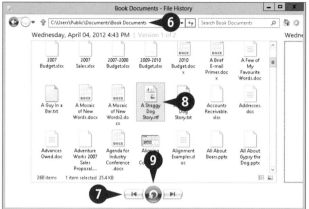

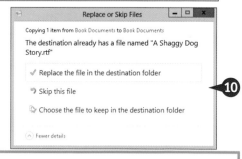

TIPS

Is it possible to restore an entire folder?

Yes, because Windows 8 also keeps track of previous versions of folders, which is useful if an entire folder becomes corrupted because of a system crash. Follow steps **1** to **7** in this section, tap the folder that you want to restore, and then tap ↻.

What should I do if I am not sure about replacing an existing file with a previous version of the file?

If you are not sure whether to replace an existing file with a previous version, tap **Choose the file to keep in the destination folder** in the Replace or Skip Files dialog box. In the File Conflict dialog box, activate the check box beside both versions (☐ changes to ☑) and then tap **Continue**. This leaves the existing file as is and restores the previous version with (2) appended to the name.

Index

Symbol
- (minus sign), 79

A
AC (Alternating Current) power, 194–195, 199
accessibility, 51
account folders, 91
accounts. *See also* user accounts
    e-mail, 82–83
    Facebook, 110–111
    Google, 116–117
    LinkedIn, 114–115
    Twitter, 112–113
Action Center, 278–279
address bars, 68
addresses
    e-mail, 84
    web, 66, 70–71
Adjust plan brightness slider, Edit Plan Settings window, 203
administrator accounts, 267, 276
alarms, battery, 200–201
albums
    music, 164–165
    photo, 140
alerts
    battery, 200–201
    Calendar app, 131
    description, 22
    event reminders, 131
    instant messages, 104
    personal information, 293
    social networks, 122–123
all-day events, 128–129
app groups, 45
app screens, 34
app settings, 34
app tiles, 6
Application Bar, 13, 34
apps
    accessing features, 58–59
    app screens, 34
    closing, 35
    description, 8–9

    freeing hard drive space, 299
    installing, 30–31
    opening e-mail attachments, 99
    overview, 26–27
    personal information, 293
    pinning, 46–47, 60–61
    restricting, 289
    searching for, 172
    Share feature, 253
    sharing data to Facebook and Twitter, 125
    starting, 32–33
    switching, 36–37
    uninstalling, 40–41
    updating, 38–39
    Windows Store, 28–29
Apps screen, 33
attachments, 88–89, 98–99
Automatic uninstalling, 41

B
backgrounds, 50–53, 139
backup copies, 231
backup histories, 308–309
bad sectors, 303
Balanced power plan, 195, 201
batteries, 199, 200–203
battery power, 194–195, 199–201
Bcc's (blind carbon copies), 85
Bing Daily page, 184–185
Bing search site, 78
Bing Weather service, 180
blocking instant messages, 105
bold text, 222–223
booting, 305, 307
brightness, screen, 198
browsing, private, 277, 290–291

C
Calendar app, 8, 128–133
calibrating screen, 208–209
Camera app, 9, 153, 263
Camera Roll folder, 150, 153
camera shake, 151
cameras, digital, 136–137

There's a Visual book for every learning level...

Simplified®

The place to start if you're new to computers. Full color.

- Computers
- Creating Web Pages
- Digital Photography
- Internet
- Mac OS
- Office
- Windows

Teach Yourself VISUALLY™

Get beginning to intermediate-level training in a variety of topics. Full color.

- Access
- Computers
- Digital Photography
- Dreamweaver
- Excel
- Flash
- HTML
- iLife
- iPhoto
- Mac OS
- Office
- Photoshop
- Photoshop Elements
- PowerPoint
- Windows
- Wireless Networking
- Word
- iPad
- iPhone
- Wordpress
- Muse

Top 100 Simplified® Tips & Tricks

Tips and techniques to take your skills beyond the basics. Full color.

- Digital Photography
- eBay
- Excel
- Google
- Internet
- Mac OS
- Office
- Photoshop
- Photoshop Elements
- PowerPoint
- Windows

...all designed for visual learners—just like you!

Master VISUALLY®

Your complete visual reference. Two-color interior.

- 3ds Max
- Creating Web Pages
- Dreamweaver and Flash
- Excel
- Excel VBA Programming
- iPod and iTunes
- Mac OS
- Office
- Optimizing PC Performance
- Photoshop Elements
- QuickBooks
- Quicken
- Windows
- Windows Mobile
- Windows Server

Visual Blueprint™

Where to go for professional-level programming instruction. Two-color interior.

- Ajax
- ASP.NET 2.0
- Excel Data Analysis
- Excel Pivot Tables
- Excel Programming
- HTML
- JavaScript
- Mambo
- PHP & MySQL
- SEO
- Ubuntu Linux
- Vista Sidebar
- Visual Basic
- XML

e **Available in print and e-book formats.**

For a complete listing of Visual books, go to wiley.com/go/visual

Visual™
An Imprint of ⓦWILEY
Now you know.